Applying Use Cases

Second Edition

The Addison-Wesley Object Technology Series

Grady Booch, Ivar Jacobson, and James Rumbaugh, Series Editors
For more information check out the series web site [http://www.awl.com/cseng/otseries/].

Armour/Miller, *Advanced Use Case Modeling: Software Systems*

Binder, *Testing Object-Oriented Systems: Models, Patterns, and Tools*

Blakley, *CORBA Security: An Introduction to Safe Computing with Objects*

Booch, *Object Solutions: Managing the Object-Oriented Project*

Booch, *Object-Oriented Analysis and Design with Applications, Second Edition*

Booch/Rumbaugh/Jacobson, *The Unified Modeling Language User Guide*

Box/Brown/Ewald/Sells, *Effective COM: 50 Ways to Improve Your COM and MTS-based Applications*

Carlson, *Modeling XML Applications with UML: Practical e-Business Applications*

Cockburn, *Surviving Object-Oriented Projects: A Manager's Guide*

Collins, *Designing Object-Oriented User Interfaces*

Conallen, *Building Web Applications with UML*

D'Souza/Wills, *Objects, Components, and Frameworks with UML: The Catalysis Approach*

Douglass, *Doing Hard Time: Developing Real-Time Systems with UML, Objects, Frameworks, and Patterns*

Douglass, *Real-Time UML, Second Edition: Developing Efficient Objects for Embedded Systems*

Fowler, *Analysis Patterns: Reusable Object Models*

Fowler/Beck/Brant/Opdyke/Roberts, *Refactoring: Improving the Design of Existing Code*

Fowler/Scott, *UML Distilled, Second Edition: A Brief Guide to the Standard Object Modeling Language*

Gomaa, *Designing Concurrent, Distributed, and Real-Time Applications with UML*

Gorton, *Enterprise Transaction Processing Systems: Putting the CORBA OTS, Encina++ and Orbix OTM to Work*

Graham, *Object-Oriented Methods, Third Edition: Principles and Practice*

Heinckiens, *Building Scalable Database Applications: Object-Oriented Design, Architectures, and Implementations*

Hofmeister/Nord/Dilip, *Applied Software Architecture*

Jacobson/Booch/Rumbaugh, *The Unified Software Development Process*

Jacobson/Christerson/Jonsson/Overgaard, *Object-Oriented Software Engineering: A Use Case Driven Approach*

Jacobson/Ericsson/Jacobson, *The Object Advantage: Business Process Reengineering with Object Technology*

Jacobson/Griss/Jonsson, *Software Reuse: Architecture, Process and Organization for Business Success*

Jordan, *C++ Object Databases: Programming with the ODMG Standard*

Kruchten, *The Rational Unified Process, An Introduction, Second Edition*

Lau, *The Art of Objects: Object-Oriented Design and Architecture*

Leffingwell/Widrig, *Managing Software Requirements: A Unified Approach*

Marshall, *Enterprise Modeling with UML: Designing Successful Software through Business Analysis*

McGregor/Sykes, *A Practical Guide to Testing Object-Oriented Software*

Mowbray/Ruh, *Inside CORBA: Distributed Object Standards and Applications*

Naiburg/Maksimchuk, *UML for Database Design*

Oestereich, *Developing Software with UML: Object-Oriented Analysis and Design in Practice*

Page-Jones, *Fundamentals of Object-Oriented Design in UML*

Pohl, *Object-Oriented Programming Using C++, Second Edition*

Pooley/Stevens, *Using UML: Software Engineering with Objects and Components*

Quatrani, *Visual Modeling with Rational Rose 2000 and UML*

Rector/Sells, *ATL Internals*

Reed, *Developing Applications with Visual Basic and UML*

Rosenberg/Scott, *Applying Use Case Driven Object Modeling with UML: An Annotated e-Commerce Example*

Rosenberg/Scott, *Use Case Driven Object Modeling with UML: A Practical Approach*

Royce, *Software Project Management: A Unified Framework*

Ruh/Herron/Klinker, *IIOP Complete: Understanding CORBA and Middleware Interoperability*

Rumbaugh/Jacobson/Booch, *The Unified Modeling Language Reference Manual*

Schneider/Winters, *Applying Use Cases, Second Edition: A Practical Guide*

Shan/Earle, *Enterprise Computing with Objects: From Client/Server Environments to the Internet*

Smith/Williams, *Performance Solutions: A Practical Guide to Creating Responsive, Scalable Software*

Warmer/Kleppe, *The Object Constraint Language: Precise Modeling with UML*

White, *Software Configuration Management Strategies and Rational ClearCase®: A Practical Introduction*

The Component Software Series

Clemens Szyperski, Series Editor
For more information check out the series web site [http://www.awl.com/cseng/csseries/].

Allen, *Realizing eBusiness with Components*

Cheesman/Daniels, *UML Components: A Simple Process for Specifying Component-Based Software*

Applying Use Cases
Second Edition

A Practical Guide

Geri Schneider

Jason P. Winters

ADDISON–WESLEY

Boston • San Francisco • New York • Toronto • Montreal
London • Munich • Paris • Madrid
Captetown • Sydney • Tokyo • Singapore • Mexico City

Many of the designations used by manufacturers and sellers to distinguish their products are claimed as trademarks. Where those designations appear in this book, and we were aware of a trademark claim, the designations have been printed in initial capital letters or in all capitals.

The authors and publisher have taken care in the preparation of this book, but make no expressed or implied warranty of any kind and assume no responsibility for errors or omissions. No liability is assumed for incidental or consequential damages in connection with or arising out of the use of the information or programs contained herein.

The publisher offers discounts on this book when ordered in quantity for special sales. For more information, please contact:

Pearson Education Corporate Sales Division
One Lake Street
Upper Saddle River, NJ 07458
(800) 382-3419
corpsales@pearsontechgroup.com

Visit AW on the Web: www.awl.com/cseng/

Library of Congress Cataloging-in-Publication Data

Schneider, Geri.
    Applying use cases : a practical guide / Geri Schneider, Jason P. Winters — 2nd ed.
        p. cm — (The Addison-Wesley object technology series)
    Includes bibliographical references and index.
    ISBN 0-201-70853-1
        1. Application software — Development. 2. Use cases (Systems engineering) I. Winters, Jason P. II. Title. III. Series.

    QA76.76.A65 S34 2001
    005.1 — dc21

                                                                            00-052165

Text printed on recycled and acid-free paper.

ISBN 0201708531

2 3 4 5 6 7 CRS 04 03 02 01

2nd Printing   June 2001

Contents

Foreword   xi

Preface to Second Edition   xiii

Preface   xv

Chapter 1   1

Getting Started

An Iterative Software Process   2
An Example Project   3
The Project Description   4
Starting Risk Analysis   6
Chapter Review   10

Chapter 2   11

Identifying System Boundaries

Identifying Actors   12
Identifying Use Cases   14
Describing Actors and Use Cases   17
Handling Time   21
Potential Boundary Problems   22
Scoping the Project   23
Chapter Review   24

Chapter 3   27

Documenting Use Cases

The Basic Use Case   27
  Pre- and Postconditions   28
  Flow of Events   29

Guidelines for Correctness and Completeness   31
Presentation Styles   32
Other Requirements   34
Handling Complex Use Cases   34
The Basic Path   35
Alternative Paths   37
Detailing Significant Behavior   40
Documenting Alternatives   42
Scenarios   47
Adding Direction to the Communicates Association   47
Chapter Review   48

Chapter 4   51

Advanced Use Case Documentation Techniques

Include   51
Extend   53
Inheritance   58
Interfaces   59
Chapter Review   65

Chapter 5   67

Diagramming Use Cases

Activity Diagrams   67
Simple Sequence Diagrams   73
Diagramming the User Interface   75
Chapter Review   77

Chapter 6   79

Level of Detail

Determining the Level of Detail   79
Traceability between Use Cases   84
Use Cases for Business Processes   85
Chapter Review   87

Chapter 7   89

Documenting Use Cases

Documentation Templates   89
Other Documents   91
Tool Support for Documents   94
Documenting Login   95
Documenting CRUD   98
Chapter Review   99

Chapter 8   101

Reviews

Review for Completeness   101
Review for Potential Problems   103
Review with End Users   103
Review with Customers   104
Review with Development   104
Reviewers   104
Adding Flexibility to Your System   105
Common Mistakes   107
   Work Flow on a Use Case Diagram   107
   Use Cases Too Small   108
   Screens as Use Cases   112
   Using Vague Terms   115
   Business versus Technical Requirements   120
Chapter Review   122

Chapter 9   123

Dividing Large Systems

Architectural Patterns   123
   Three-Tier Architectural Pattern   124
   Pipe and Filter Architectural Pattern   125
   Object-Oriented Architectural Pattern   126
   Order-Processing Architecture Example   126
Testing the Architecture with Use Cases   129
Sequence Diagrams   133
Defining Interfaces between Subsystems   133
Subordinate Use Cases   136

Creating Subsystem Documentation   140
Subordinate versus Alternative versus Include   141
Chapter Review   142

Chapter 10   143

Use Cases and the Project Plan

Planning the Project   143
    Build versus Buy Decisions   149
    Prototyping   150
Estimating Work with Use Cases   151
    Weighting Actors   151
    Weighting Use Cases   152
    Weighting Technical Factors   153
    Use Case Points   157
    Project Estimate   157
Chapter Review   158

Chapter 11   159

Constructing and Delivering a System

Key Abstractions of the Domain   159
    Identifying Key Abstractions in Use Cases   160
    Diagramming Scenarios with Key Abstractions   161
    Diagramming Key Abstractions   163
    Use Case versus Subsystem View   164
The Iteration Schedule   166
Delivery and Beyond   167
    User Guides and Training   168
    Sales Kits and Marketing Literature   168
    Use Cases After Delivery   168
Chapter Review   169
Final Wrap-Up   170

Appendix A   171

Resources

Appendix B   175

Documentation Templates

System or Subsystem Documents   175
Use Case Document   176

Appendix C   179

UML Notation

Appendix D   185

Sending Results of the Use Case Estimator

Appendix E   187

Order-Processing System

Order-Processing System   188
  Risk Factors   *188*
System-Level Use Cases   189
Architecture   190

Index   239

Foreword

When I first proposed a new set of modeling concepts back in 1967 as the result of my work on large telecommunication switching systems and system design, the idea of use cases as a method of analysis was very sketchy. With the emergence of object-oriented ideas and my subsequent work in applying OO in the 1980s and formalizing the principles underlying Objectory, use case analysis began to take better shape and to play a significant role in the analysis of the problem domain. Today the ideas embodied in use cases have matured, and this technique has become a significant tool that belongs in every analyst's toolkit.

With the incorporation of use cases into the industry standard modeling language, UML, it is time for a new book that illustrates the current notation and semantics of use cases in a practical, easy-to-understand manner. Use case analysis also plays a central role in the new Unified Process for software development. It is, therefore, critical that managers, architects, designers, analysts, domain experts, programmers, and testers understand how to apply use cases.

In *Applying Use Cases*, Geri Schneider and Jason Winters have done an excellent job of introducing this powerful technique and demonstrating its application in real-world settings. Rather than making everything perfect up front, the examples progress in much the same manner you would find in a real project, with early rough models being refined as the team gains understanding of the project. This realism allows the introduction of issues that would arise in actual projects. *Applying Use Cases* is easy to read, but contains a wealth of detail.

This book clearly reflects Geri's experience as a trainer for Rational Software, the time she has spent mentoring and training customers of Wyyzzk Training and Consulting, and the time Jason has spent using the techniques and mentoring engineers at Lucent Technologies. It is an excellent resource for anyone who needs to understand use case analysis, and I recommend it highly.

Ivar Jacobson

Preface to the Second Edition

There have been many changes for us and for the UML since the first edition was released in September 1998. The book has changed to stay current.

The material in the first edition is also in the second edition, but you may find it in a new location. We moved the engineering-oriented material to the end of the book, and the business-oriented material to the beginning. This should make it easier for different audiences to find the material that interests them.

We updated the book to UML 1.3. A lot of the changes are in Chapters 3 and 4 because that is where we described most of the notation. The uses relationship became two relationships in UML 1.3, include and generalization. The extends relationship became extend. In both cases the notation changed as well. The definition of scenarios changed a bit too. What we used to call scenarios are now called paths.

We have added some new material that we found useful and important. Chapter 6 is a new chapter on setting the level of detail in use cases. This includes information on business process-level use cases and maintaining traceability between use cases at different levels of detail. Chapter 7, Documenting Use Cases, includes some ideas on handling login and CRUD (create, read, update, delete) in use cases. Chapter 8, Reviews, has a new section on common mistakes we have seen and how to fix them. We have included more information on sequence diagrams in Chapters 5 and 9.

There have been changes for me and Jason as well. Jason left Octel and is now a staff engineer at Cadence Design Systems. I liked having my own business, but didn't like the bookkeeping, so I took a job running the OO division of Andrews Technology, Inc. We still have Wyyzzk and Jason does some weekend consulting for that business. Things even changed on the publishing side. Addison-Wesley is now part of Pearson Education, and we have a whole new team managing the Object Technology series. They have been wonderful to work with and made the transition as smooth as possible.

One question we get asked a lot is: What do the footprints and people talking icons mean? The footprints mark major steps in the process. The people talking appear next to the storyline.

Thank you for all the e-mail about the book. We don't always get a chance to reply, but we have read all your letters and hope we have answered most of your questions in this second edition.

Many thanks to our distinguished reviewers. They worked as hard as we did to make this book happen:

- Lauren Thayer
- Venkat Narayanan
- Guy Rish
- Kelli A. Houston, Rational Software Corporation
- John Sunda Hsia

Speaking of hard workers, we were most fortunate to be working with Paul Becker, Ross Venables, Tyrrell Albaugh, and her production team at Addison-Wesley. Our most heartfelt thanks for all your support and patience. You guys did all the tough work to make this book a reality.

Finally, a few very special people. Thanks to Lauren Thayer and Kristy Hughes for being my constant friends for almost 15 years. And my cats, Patches and Joker, for keeping me company all those hours on the computer. And as always, thank you to Jason Winters for his love, support, and encouragement. You all are the wind beneath my wings.

Geri Schneider Winters
Santa Clara, California

Preface

You're about to start a new project. Sometimes it seems like colonizing the moon would be easier. But you assemble a stalwart team and prepare to set sail on the good ship *Requirements,* hoping to reach the fabled land of Success. They say there are no failed projects in Success, and the profit margin is so high, the streets are paved with gold.

There are many dangers between here and Success. Many a ship is sunk on the way—some say as many as 80 percent never reach that fabled land. You query those who have tried before. "Use a ship from the OO line," they say. "Booch, OMT, OOSE, UML are all good models to choose from. You'll also need a chart showing risks along the way and an architecture of the major land masses. And finally you'll need to plot a course of use cases to reach your destination."

Use Cases are included in the Unified Modeling Language and are used throughout the Rational Unified Process. They are gaining wide acceptance in many different businesses and industries. Most often, use cases are applied to software projects and enterprise-wide applications.

This book is for anyone interested in applying use cases to project development. While we can't guarantee you will always have successful projects when using use cases, we can give you another way of looking at the projects you are developing and some tools that will make success more likely.

You will get more benefit out of the book if you have some basic knowledge of object-oriented concepts. We will use the Unified Modeling Language for the notation, explaining the notation as we use it. A good book to use for reference on the notation is *UML Distilled* by Fowler. This is an excellent book on the topic and easy to read.

This book is organized using the Rational Unified Process as a framework. Within the phases of the process, we talk about the activities in the phase, focusing on activities based on use cases. We touch lightly on activities that interact with use cases, such as software architecture, project management, and object-oriented analysis and design. These are very important activities, with whole books devoted to each topic. Therefore, in the resource list in Appendix A, you will find our favorite books on these topics.

We have used one example, an order-processing system for a mail order company, throughout the book. This allows us to maintain consistency and build up a reasonably complex example. Parts of the solution are given in the various chapters to illustrate the concepts.

This book is presented as a sequence of steps, though life is never that simple. Each part will contribute to the rest until the system is complete. So if a section says to create an architecture, do what you can at that time, using what you currently know. You will add to it and refine it based on knowledge gained while working through the process.

You don't have to read the whole book before starting with use cases. Chapters 1 through 6 give the basics of working with use cases. We recommend that everyone reads those chapters. Chapter 9 covers architecture and mapping use cases into the architecture. Chapter 7 covers documenting use cases. Chapter 10 covers project planning with use cases, and Chapter 8 covers reviewing the use case documents. Chapter 11 goes into moving from use cases to OOAD.

Ultimately, use cases are about documenting your system. Plan on doing a lot of writing. Appendix A provides a list of books we reference throughout the text, as well as other books we have found useful when developing projects. Appendix B shows the document templates used. These provide an example and a starting point for your own project. Modify them as needed to work with your project.

△ ▽ △ ▽ △

In October of 1995, Rational Software Corporation merged with Objective Systems. Among other things, this merger brought with it Ivar Jacobson and his use cases. In February 1996, I wrote and delivered the first use case course for Rational, which combined use cases with the object-oriented methodologies of Grady Booch and Jim Rumbaugh. Since that time, I have taught and run workshops on use cases with many of Rational's customers, as well as customers of my consulting company, Wyyzzk Training and Consulting. As I have taught them, so they have taught me. This book came out of what I've learned through the workshops.

Chapter 1

Getting Started

Use cases are used to describe the outwardly visible requirements of a system. They are used in the requirements analysis phase of a project and contribute to test plans and user guides. They are used to create and validate a proposed design and to ensure it meets all requirements. Use cases also are used when creating a project schedule, helping to plan what goes into each release.

This book will give practical guidelines for applying use cases to a project. We will cover a project from its initial inception ("Hey! How about. . . .") to just before we actually start to build a system. We also will look at applying use cases in testing the system code and creating user manuals.

In this book we'll look at use cases from many viewpoints, showing how they contribute to the architecture, scheduling, requirements, testing, and documentation of a project. We'll look at the system from the user's point of view, discuss issues such as boundaries, interfaces, and scoping, and look at how to break a really large system into manageable chunks. We also will look at who would be interested in the documentation you'll be writing and what to look for in a review. We need to consider things such as how to build flexibility into a system, how to make a build-versus-buy decision, and how to turn the documents into an object-oriented design.

This book does not contain in-depth details about software architecture, project planning, testing, process, or methodology. Instead, you will find a listing of books we like on these topics in Resources (Appendix A). There are a number of good books on these topics; the resource list gives you just a starting point.

AN ITERATIVE SOFTWARE PROCESS

Use cases can be used in many processes. Our favorite is a process that is iterative and risk driven. It works well with use cases and object-oriented methodologies. It helps identify and address risks early in the process, leading to more robust and better quality systems. One commonly used iterative and risk driven process is the Rational Unified Process (RUP). We will give a very brief description of RUP here, showing where use cases fit into the process. Subsequent chapters will go into more detail on how use cases are used at each phase.

RUP is divided into four primary phases: inception, elaboration, construction, and transition.

During the inception phase you will determine the scope of the project and create a business case for it. At the end of the inception phase you should be able to answer the question, Does it make good business sense for us to continue with this project?

During the elaboration phase you will do requirements analysis and risk analysis, develop a baseline architecture, and create a plan for the construction phase.

During the construction phase you will progress through a series of iterations. Each iteration will include analysis, design, implementation, and testing.

During the transition phase you will complete the things that make what you developed into a product. These can include beta testing, performance tuning, and creating additional documentation such as training, user guides, and sales kits. You will create a plan for rolling out the product to the user community, whether internal or external.

So where do use cases fit into all this? In the inception phase, high-level use cases are developed to help scope out the project: What should be included in this project, and what belongs to another project? What can you realistically accomplish given your schedule and budget?

In the elaboration phase, you will develop more detailed use cases. These will contribute to the risk analysis and the baseline architecture. The use cases will be used to create the plan for the construction phase.

In the construction phase, you will use use cases as a starting point for design and for developing test plans. More detailed use cases may be developed as part of the analysis of each iteration. Use cases provide some of the requirements that have to be satisfied for each iteration.

In the transition phase, you will use use cases to develop user guides and training.

AN EXAMPLE PROJECT

Throughout this book we will use an example project. We will work through all the techniques using the same example. The notation we will use is the Unified Modeling Language (UML), which is outlined in Appendix C.

The example we will be following is for an order-processing system for a mail order company. Let's start at the very beginning, when four friends gather around a table after dinner and someone gets an idea.

"This is crazy!" Dennis exclaimed, sitting down next to Tara, almost spilling his coffee.

"What is?" Lisa asked, sitting down with Gus and her own cup of mocha.

"The fact that I can't find a single supplier that will give me reasonable service and parts without all the headaches! I've got one supplier who has great service, and I like dealing with him. But he takes three weeks to get me even the simplest order! And the other one—oh, they're something else. Sure, I can get orders within three days, but half the time the orders are wrong, and when I call them back about it, they make it sound like it's my fault! It's almost as if they are *trying* to make me go elsewhere."

"Yes, I know what you mean," Lisa said. "I've had my own problems with mail order companies. You'd think they would pay more attention to their customers!"

"I really think I could do a better job myself. I sure know a lot about what not to do."

This had been a common complaint from Dennis in the last several months, and by now the group was well acquainted with it. Tara suddenly smiled and piped up with "Why don't you start one?" "Start one what?" Dennis muttered into in his coffee.

"Start a mail order company! What would you do to fix the problems you've seen?"

"Well, it seems like automating the order processing would help a lot. It would also let me run the company myself for a while. But I don't know anything about software."

At this point, Gus joined the conversation. "You need to plan it out. I learned a method in my OO class we could use. And we could help! By putting us and all of our experiences together, we could figure out how to use our different skills in the right places and work out the sections we don't know!"

"OO? What's that? You know I'm not a programmer. I don't know anything about programming languages."

"No, OO isn't about a programming language. It's a way of thinking about a problem, a way of modeling and breaking it down into identifiable objects so you can work with them. It really doesn't matter what the problem is, whether it's a programming problem or a problem like starting a new business. It's just an approach on how you look at it."

"Hmmm. . . ." mused Dennis, liking the idea the more he thought about it. "And you would all be willing to help?"

"Sure!"

"Why not?"

"Sounds like fun!"

"Well . . . okay! So, Gus, where do we start with this all-dancing-all-singing magical OO process?"

Before you can write use cases, you have to gather some information that will provide a starting point. This is part of the inception phase of the RUP. The information you collect includes a project description, market factors that affect your project, risk factors for your project, and assumptions you are making. The rest of this chapter will touch on all these sources of information.

THE PROJECT DESCRIPTION

So you have an idea for a project. The next step is to write out a description of what you plan to do. It sounds simple, and it can be. But the larger the group you have writing this description, the longer it will take and the more complex it will be. It is best to have just a couple of people write out a brief, but complete, description of the project.

The project description should range in size from one short paragraph for a small project up to no more than a couple of pages for a really large project. This is not a description of the requirements, but a description of the project in general.

The biggest mistake made at this point is not writing the description. Usually this is because everybody thinks they know what the project is about, so why write it down? We have spent several days in meetings while the project team has argued about what a one-paragraph description should say. Until you write it out, you can't be sure everyone agrees on the same project description.

"So, let's get started. We need to write out a description of order processing in normal everyday language. This will become the problem statement, a way to start getting the requirements for the project."

"Why do we need to write it out? We're all familiar with ordering products from mail order companies. This seems too formal for such a simple problem."

"Well, we should write it all down to make sure everyone has the same idea. Even if you're working alone, it's still a good idea to write it down so you don't leave out something important. Besides, it'll give us someplace to start, and we can add to it as we go along. Here, I'll start."

Problem Description

We are developing order-processing software for a mail order company called National Widgets, which is a reseller of products purchased from various suppliers.

Twice a year the company publishes a catalog of products, which is mailed to customers and other interested people.

"You think twice a year is good? What if our products change faster than that?"

"Remember, this is just to start us off. We will add to it and change it as we get farther along and understand more about what's going on. Let's keep going."

More Requirements

Customers purchase products by submitting a list of products with payment to National Widgets. National Widgets fills the order and ships the products to the customer's address.

The order-processing software tracks the order from the time it is received until the product is shipped.

National Widgets provides quick service. They should be able to ship a customer's order by the fastest, most efficient means possible.

"Great! That looks like us! Now, what else should we do?"

What did our friends do right? They kept the description brief, talking about what they want to accomplish, not how to do it. They wrote down the elements important to them: It's a catalog company—a reseller, not a manufacturer; it provides quick service; and the software is used throughout the process to track orders. These are the key characteristics of their project. They haven't worried about making their description perfect. If there were something that they should NOT do, they would have written that down as well. They now have a basic description that they agree on but that may need to be modified later. However, the key characteristics should not change.

STARTING RISK ANALYSIS

Now that you have a description, the next step is to write down other things you know about your project. You are looking for marketing factors that will influence your project, good or bad, and anything that could cause the project to fail or to be rejected by the customer. We will use these with the problem statement to create use cases, other requirements, and risk factors. Start by considering market factors:

- Who or what the competition is
- What technologies you are depending on, such as:
  - Web
  - Object databases
  - Power PC chip
- Market trends that influence your project
- Future trends you are depending on, such as:
  - More home offices
  - More small companies
- Is it possible to be:
  - Not fast enough to market
  - Too fast to market

For our mail order company we can create a list of market factors based on personal experience.

Mail Order Market Factors

In most households, all adults work at least part-time. They have less time available for shopping, so they usually are willing to pay for conveniences such as purchase delivery.

Web shopping and home-shopping networks are popular and are competitors in this market.

Other mail order companies provide 24-hour order takers, delivery times ranging from overnight to two weeks, gift wrap, and volume discounts.

Be creative as you make this list. Brainstorm a lot. Put down just about anything you can think of. Put down the wildly unlikely as well as things that will probably happen. The idea at this stage is to look at the project from many viewpoints. This will help solidify your ideas. Look at some books on marketing trends for ideas. What are competing companies doing right or doing wrong?

You also need to consider risk factors in your project. You need to include things that can go wrong. Writing down only the things that you'd *like* to happen is a sure recipe for disaster. It is far better to think of how things can go wrong so you can plan for them than to wander along and be surprised.

You also need to include the possibility of being wildly successful. Sometimes you'll find that things actually can go wrong if you are too successful. For example, what would happen to National Widgets if, in the first month, they get 4,000 calls? They will now have to handle multiple order takers and large amounts of data. Presuming the company can handle this surge, can the software handle it? The company could lose business if the software is not up to the demands placed on it, possibly getting a bad reputation because of it. Our friends will write this down as one of their risks.

Here are some things to consider as possible risk factors:

- People
  - Team not experienced
  - Team not familiar with the technologies to be used
  - Unable to hire people with the right background
- System
  - Number of transactions per time frame
  - Number of expected users
  - Expected duration of some functionality
  - Legacy systems you have to interface with, such as:
    - Software
    - Business processes
    - Data stores, databases
- Resource
  - Too short a schedule
  - Too many users
  - Supplier can't or won't deliver product we depend on
- Technology
  - Dependence on a technology that changes
- Corporate
  - Lack of user acceptance
  - Too fast company growth

Our risk factors for the order-processing project take into consideration the inexperience of the team, system failure, and the needs of the market.

National Widgets Risk Factors

- Some of the people designing the software are inexperienced.
- How can we prevent lost orders on system failure?
- The system has to be easy for nontechnical people to use.
- Can we be successful if we don't support a Web interface?
- What if the system is immediately flooded with orders?
- How do we handle many simultaneous users in different parts of the company?
- How do we handle the database crashing?

Take this list of risks and the list of market factors, eliminate extremes such as a comet crashing into your company and putting you out of business or the sun failing to rise, and prioritize the rest. The new prioritized list you've created is your first risk analysis. All the things you've listed on it put you at risk for not completing your project. The more serious items are listed first, with less severe risks at the bottom. The high-risk factors must be addressed if you expect your project to succeed.

Looking at National Widgets risk factors, we want to mark the items high risk if we are fairly sure we will fail unless those risks are addressed, and we are fairly certain that these risks will happen. We chose three risks as high risk for this project: lack of team experience, ease of use for nontechnical people, and support for a Web interface. We picked one medium risk: the need for multiple users to access the system at the same time. This is a real need, but there are many good technical solutions to the problem, some of which we could just purchase and incorporate into our system. This is less likely to cause project failure than lack of team experience. The other risk factors we marked low. The system flooded with orders is judged to be highly unlikely for this company, and the database or system crashing should be fairly unlikely as well. Experience suggests that if an order gets lost, the customer is likely to call us looking for it, so we can recover data that way.

You may pick the priorities differently. Each company and project will have different ways of looking at the problem, different factors that are important. Also, remember that this is just a starting point and that you'll be adding to it as you continue.

As part of your risk list, put together and maintain a list of assumptions. These are decisions you make with little or no hard data. You may need to pick one way of doing something based on gut feel or experience. Record that decision and why you made it. This list should be reviewed regularly. Some things will remain as assumptions. For others, you will be able to get hard data on which to base your decisions. Remove things that are no longer assumptions and add the new assumptions you've made.

Let's go back and see how the group members are doing with their lists.

"Okay, it's been a busy evening. Let's see what we've gotten out of it." Gus handed around the lists shown in Exhibit 1-1.

"Wow," said Dennis. "We sure can fail in a lot of ways. But how has this helped us define the software? So far, all it's done is make me worry that we forgot something."

"Don't worry, Dennis. We're just getting started. We want to find things that could make us fail now so we can fix the problems rather than being surprised by them later."

Exhibit 1-1 Order-Processing Problem Statement

Problem Description

- We are developing order-processing software for a mail order company called National Widgets, which is a reseller of products purchased from various suppliers.
- Twice a year the company publishes a catalog of products, which is mailed to customers and other interested people.
- Customers purchase products by submitting a list of products with payment to National Widgets. National Widgets fills the order and ships the products to the customer's address.
- The order-processing software tracks the order from the time it is received until the product is shipped.
- National Widgets will provide quick service. They should be able to ship a customer's order by the fastest, most efficient means possible.
- Customers may return items for restocking but will sometimes pay a fee.

Assumptions

- An electronic interface, such as the Web, would be good for some customers.
- We expect to use multiple shipping companies and insured methods.

Risk Factors

- *High:*
- Some of the people designing the software are inexperienced.
- The system has to be easy for nontechnical people to use.
- Can we be successful if we don't support a Web interface?

- *Medium:*
- How do we handle many simultaneous users in different parts of the company?
- *Low:*
- How can we prevent lost orders on system failure?
- What if the system is immediately flooded with orders?
- How do we handle the database crashing?

Exhibit 1-1 Order-Processing Problem Statement (*Continued*)

Market Factors

- In most households, all adults work at least part-time. They have less time available for shopping, so are usually willing to pay for conveniences such as purchase delivery.
- Web shopping and home shopping networks are popular and are competitors in this market.
- Other mail order companies provide 24-hour order takers, delivery times ranging from overnight to two weeks, gift wrap, and volume discounts.

CHAPTER REVIEW

Table 1-1 shows deliverables you should have completed at this point. Your risk analysis should include known risks, other known market factors, and assumptions you have made about the project.

These are just preliminary versions, showing what you know right now. You will modify these things as you learn more about your project. The next chapter covers using use cases to find the boundaries of the system and the scope of the project.

Table 1-1 Inception Phase Deliverables

Complete	Deliverables
✔	Project description
✔	Risk analysis
	Use case diagram
	Description of actors and use cases
	Project proposal

Chapter 2

Identifying System Boundaries

By now you have a high-level overview of the project and an idea of the risks you are facing. Let's define a couple of terms we have been using before going on. The system is whatever you are planning to create. It could be software, hardware, or processes. The project encompasses all the things you do to build a system. So it will include things such as planning, scheduling, and documentation.

The next step in our process is to clearly identify the boundaries of the system. This means finding out what things are inside your system (you have to worry about creating them) and what are outside your system (you don't have to create them, but you have to worry about interfacing with them). You should also be concerned with scoping the project. This involves defining what parts of the system you will create within a certain time period, on a certain budget.

Some system boundaries are very easy to define, such as a person interacting with a program. Most likely you won't have to worry about creating the person. The program, however, is clearly within your project. Other boundaries have fuzzier borders.

System Boundary Example

What is the boundary of this system?

National Widgets needs to ship orders to customers. Shipping needs to include packaging and labeling orders, weighing them, and determining postage based on shipping method, speed of delivery, insurance, weight, destination, and so on.

Should our order-processing system include calculating postage?

You will find the boundaries of your system by identifying the actors and the use cases.

IDENTIFYING ACTORS

We'll start off by identifying the actors in our system. Actors are anything that interfaces with your system—for example, people, other software, hardware devices, data stores, or networks. Each actor defines a particular role. Each entity outside your system may be represented by one or more actors. So one physical person may be represented by several actors because that person takes on different roles with regard to the system. Or several physical people might be represented by one actor because they all take on the same role with regard to the system.

For example, a person, Mary Smith, is a customer of National Widgets. But she also is an employee of National Widgets. Thus, Mary Smith is represented by two actors, Customer and Employee, because they represent two different roles with regard to the company. John Forsythe also is a customer of National Widgets. He and Mary Smith are represented by the same actor, Customer, because they take on the same role with regard to the company.

Actors are always external to your system. They are never a part of your system. To help find actors in your system, look for things in the categories of people, other software, hardware devices, data stores, or networks. You also might find it useful to ask questions such as:

- Who uses the system?
- Who installs the system?
- Who starts up the system?
- Who maintains the system?
- Who shuts down the system?
- What other systems use this system?
- Who gets information from this system?
- Who provides information to the system?
- Does anything happen automatically at a preset time?

Gus and his friends have had some time to get the general feel of what they want the software to do. Now it's time to put some of those ideas to use.

"Well," Gus said. "Here we are again. That was a great dinner, Tara! Thanks!"

"You're welcome, Gus. I guess Dennis didn't notice. He's got that faraway look in his eyes. Hello? Dennis? Hey!"

"Huh? Oh! Sorry, gang. I was just thinking about what we ended up doing last week. I still don't see how it's helped us so far, other than giving us a very basic description of what we're doing. Don't we need a lot more details? I just don't get it."

"Well," Gus said, "you're right. We're ready for the next step in the process—figuring out who we interact with."

"Don't we interact with customers?" Lisa asked as she sat down with her coffee.

"Yes, we do! And that's why we call the customer an actor. In fact, the customer will be the first actor that we write down. Who else? Tara?"

"Well, since we have to get orders from us to our customers, we'll need to interact with someone like Dolphin Mail or the Postal Service."

"Good!" Gus exclaimed. "Now let's put that down on paper."

Dennis, glancing at the drawing, said, "Hey! That guy even looks like one of our customers!"

"Yes, that helps us keep in mind who's doing what. The stick men are our actors. What's wrong, Lisa?"

"Why is there only one shipping company? Won't we work with a lot of companies?"

"That's right. But fortunately, we don't show each person or each shipping company as a separate actor. For example, we might use Federal Express, DHL, or Dolphin Mail for deliveries. Because they all interface with us the same way, we can show them as one actor."

"There he goes, talking 'interfaces' again . . . ," Lisa muttered.

"Well, it's true, they *are* using the same interface. For example, what if we had to have a different type of order form for each customer? Wouldn't *that* be a headache!"

"It sure would! Okay, you've convinced me."

"Are we really interfacing with the shipping companies? That would be only if they used our order-processing system directly, right?"

"Say, that's right. Wouldn't it really be a shipping clerk at National Widgets using the software?"

"And our customer should be a customer service rep."

"What about the Web? Don't we want to interact with customers directly?"

Gus stepped in. "Let's go ahead and put them all down. [See Exhibit 2-1.] We can change this later if we decide to do or not do some of those things."

Exhibit 2-1 Order-Processing Actors

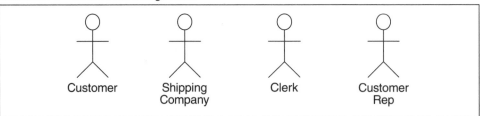

Customer   Shipping Company   Clerk   Customer Rep

IDENTIFYING USE CASES

The next step is to go through all of the actors and identify use cases for each one. A use case is a behavior of the system that produces a measurable result of value to an actor. Use cases describe the things actors want the system to do, such as querying the status of an existing order. A use case should be a complete task from the actor's perspective. The behavior of a single use case is often complete in a relatively short period of time. If parts of the use case are widely separated in time, especially if they are performed by different actors, then those parts are probably better as separate use cases.

In the UML, a use case is always started by an actor. We have found it useful on occasion to initiate use cases from inside the system, but this is rare.

Ask yourself:

- What functions will the actor want from the system?
- Does the system store information? What actors will create, read, update, or delete that information?
- Does the system need to notify an actor about changes in its internal state?
- Are there any external events that the system must know about? What actor informs the system about those events?

Other kinds of use cases to consider are startup, shutdown, diagnostics, installation, training, and changing a business process. A common one that many people forget is maintenance. How are you going to repair the system? Will you have to shut it down or can you do your maintenance while still using the system? When considering these and other questions, determine whether these functions are handled by your system or performed by another system. If these functions are handled by another system, that system is a potential actor to your system. All of the use cases together will describe the complete functionality of the system from the user's point of view.

"Okay," Gus said. "Any more ideas for actors? No? Well, that's okay. We have enough information to get started with the next step, which is identifying use cases. We can add more actors later as we find them."

"So," Dennis asked, "what is a use case?"

"It's a way actors use our system," Gus replied. "So, what do our customers want from us?"

"Hmm . . ." Tara mused. "Well, I would assume they want to place an order. If they don't, we won't be in business long enough to worry about anything else!"

"Great. What else do our customers want?"

"They check the status of their order."

"They have to get our catalog to know what to order!"

"They cancel an order."

"Pessimist."

"They return stuff they've purchased."

"Hey, what happens after they order? Don't they have to receive the order?"

"Whoa! Slow down! I can't write that fast!" Gus quickly jotted down notes and soon was ready to go on. "Who asked about what happens after they order? Lisa? Okay, what does happen after they order?"

"Well, I would imagine we'd ship the order to them. Hey! Does that mean that we need to notify the shipping company when an order is ready for delivery?"

"Very good!" Gus said. "That's exactly what it means. So now we have to add that use case for the shipping company actor. Let's add the use cases to our diagram [see Exhibit 2-2]. We can use a single actor to show the starting point of many operations, such as checking the status of an order or canceling it. The use cases are represented by ovals on the diagram. The boundary of the system is represented by a rectangle containing the use cases and the name of the system. Actors are outside the rectangle because they are outside the system. Solid lines connect actors to their use cases."

"Hey!" Tara pointed at the page. "Do we really want the supplier interfacing directly with our software?"

"Maybe we can get the software to automatically place an order with a supplier when our stock is low."

"Shouldn't the inventory system do that?"

"Are we writing that too?"

"No way. It's enough to just process orders. We can buy an inventory system to use."

"Isn't that an actor, then?"

Exhibit 2-2 Order-Processing Use Cases

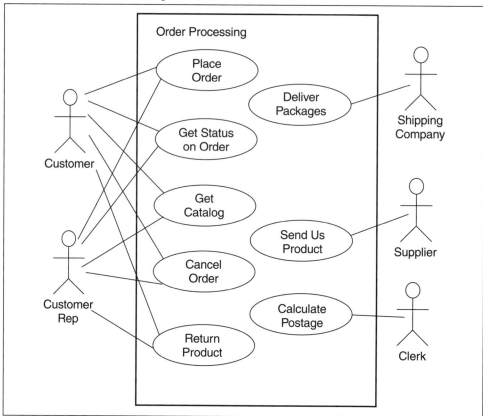

"You're right. How about accounting systems?"

"Sure. Buy that too."

"I have a question for you, Gus," Lisa said. "How do you know where to draw the circles versus the actor? Why don't we have an actor in place of the Deliver Packages use case? Doesn't the Place Order use case interact with it? Wouldn't that make Deliver Packages an actor?"

"Not exactly. You see, one of the basic rules for something to be declared an actor is that we don't have control over it. If we don't have control over something, then it's an outside influence, as in outside our process, and that means it's an actor. If we have full control of it, like we do between the Place Order module and the Deliver Packages module, then it's internal to our system. We don't need to define the interface between Place Order and Deliver Packages yet because nobody on the outside can see it. Only the interface between Deliver Packages and a Shipping Company is visible."

"Got it! Let's keep going, because I've got some more use cases for you."

DESCRIBING ACTORS AND USE CASES

Each actor and use case needs a descriptive name and a brief description that is one or two sentences long. Include these with your use case diagram.

Order-Processing Actor Descriptions

Customer—a person who orders products from National Widgets

Customer rep—an employee of National Widgets who processes customer requests

Shipping company—USPS, UPS, DHL, FedEx, DM, and so on

Clerk—an employee of National Widgets who packages, labels, and ships orders

Inventory system—software that tracks the company inventory

Accounting system—software that keeps the company books

In the process of identifying and defining actors and use cases, you are determining your system boundaries—what is inside the system (use cases) and what is outside (actors). Record this information in a use case diagram. Remember, this is only the first cut! Throughout this process, we will be constantly adding to and refining this diagram.

Order-Processing Use Case Descriptions

Place Order—a customer creates a new order to request products and provide payment for those products.

Get Catalog—a customer requests a catalog.

Get Status on Order—a customer gets the status of an existing order.

Return Product—a customer returns a product for a refund.

Cancel Order—a customer cancels an existing order.

Register Complaint—a customer sends a message to customer support.

Deliver Packages—we request a shipping company to deliver products to our customers.

Calculate Postage—determine how much postage is needed to send an order to a customer.

Print Mailing Label—print a mailing label for an order.

Get Product Information—get information about a product, it's price and quantity in stock.

Update Product Quantities—update the amount of product in stock.

Receive Back-ordered Items—the processing we need to do when items that are back-ordered have been received.

Charge Account—charge a customer's account.

Credit Account—credit a customer's account.

Review your system description, market factors, risk factors, assumptions, and any other requirements you are aware of. Are all the users of the system represented as actors? Are all the system functions represented as use cases?

What Gus and his friends have for a use case diagram at this point is represented in Exhibit 2-3. They have come up with things that are done by actors

Exhibit 2-3 Order-Processing Use Cases

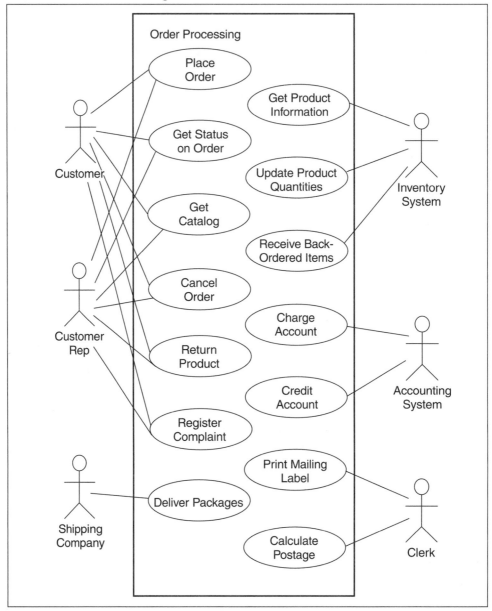

representing the customer, customer rep, shipping company, clerk, inventory system, and accounting system.

What if the use case diagram is too big and messy? Then create several use case diagrams. Each diagram might represent a major area of functionality in your system. In a large system, you could create packages representing subsystems or areas of major functionality. A package in the UML is a container for other UML elements. Then make a use case diagram for each package, showing the use cases it contains (Exhibits 2-4, 2-5, and 2-6).

Exhibit 2-4   Order-Processing Use Case Packages

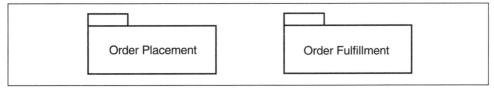

Exhibit 2-5   Order Placement Use Cases

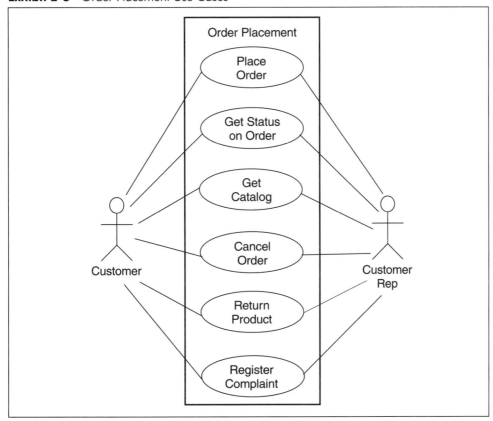

Exhibit 2-6 Order Fulfillment Use Cases

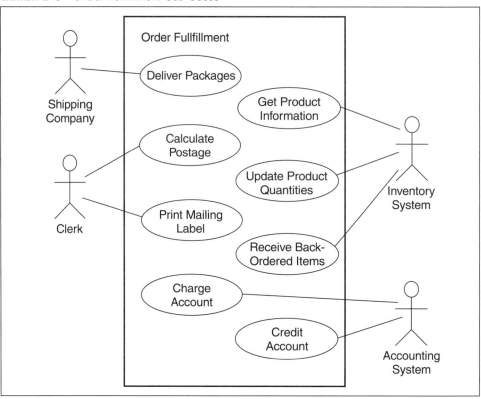

You could have one use case diagram per actor or per use case. We like creating a context diagram for each use case, showing all the elements it interacts with (see Exhibit 2-7).

At various points in the project, you need to compare these diagrams to remove redundancies and keep them consistent. Automated Computer-Aided Software Engineering (CASE) tools can help with this process.

Exhibit 2-7 Place Order Context Diagram

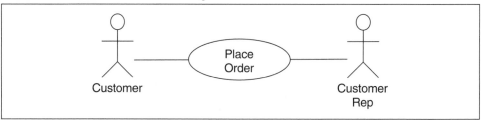

HANDLING TIME

In some systems, certain activities take place at certain times. For example, we might run payroll every Friday or print a system report every day at midnight. In the order-processing system we might want to automatically send out catalogs once a quarter. There are essentially two ways to handle time in use cases.

One method is to treat time as an actor. Then, the time actor can initiate the use case to run the payroll, print the system report, or send a catalog once a quarter (Exhibit 2-8).

The second method of handling time is to treat it as part of the system. In this method, a use case starts itself at some time. The actor that interacts with the use case is one that will receive the output of the use case. You might define a paymaster actor to receive the output of the Run Payroll use case. Possibly a printer actor receives the output of the Print System Report use case. A customer receives the output of sending catalogs (see Exhibit 2-9). Of course, you can combine these methods (see Exhibit 2-10).

Exhibit 2-8   Time as an Actor

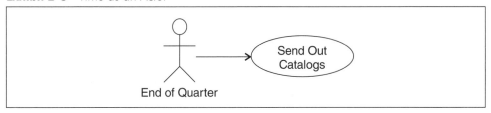

Exhibit 2-9   Actor Receiving Automatically Generated Output from System

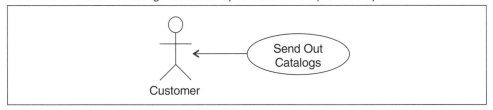

Exhibit 2-10   Combining Methods

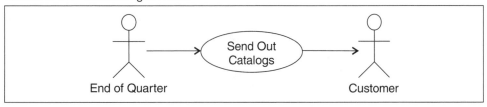

POTENTIAL BOUNDARY PROBLEMS

What if some of your requirements should be handled by one of the actors? In this case, you need to determine if that actor is really a part of your system. If not, then the requirements cannot be a part of the system. In this case, the requirements must be communicated to the actor or whoever is designing the system represented by that actor. Otherwise, the requirements need to be redefined so it is clear they are a part of the system.

If you decide the actor should be part of your system, look at the description. Perhaps the actor or its role needs to be redefined to make the system boundary clearer. If the actor becomes a part of your system, what about use cases that were associated with that actor? Who or what interacts with those use cases now? Maybe the use cases need to be redefined.

Who Handles This Requirement?

National Widgets decides they need to provide insurance on the packages they ship. Who will provide this insurance? Will National Widgets provide the insurance, or will the shipping companies provide the insurance? Will the insurance be tracked in the order-processing system or calculated by the system? How does the system decide which kind of insurance to use, or should it?

What if you find new requirements as you go through the process of identifying actors and use cases? Ask yourself if the requirements are inside or outside your system. Some of the questions to ask yourself when you find new requirements are:

- Are these requirements necessary for this system?
- Are these requirements something this system would logically do?
- How do the new requirements affect our current risk analysis?
- Can these requirements be handled by one of the current actors to our system? In other words, is someone else responsible for these requirements?
- Are these requirements something our customers would expect our system to do?
- Would these requirements differentiate our product in the marketplace?

Defining a clear boundary for your system may be very difficult. That would indicate your system is not well defined. If you expect to deliver a system on time and on budget, you must have a good project description with well-defined system boundaries. It is worth spending the time doing this work up front. Otherwise, you will struggle with it throughout the lifetime of the project.

SCOPING THE PROJECT

 Having determined the boundaries of your system, you need to decide on a scope for your project. A project has particular begin and end dates and some amount of money that can be spent to accomplish the goals of the project. Do you intend to build the whole system in the current project? If not, you need to clearly define the pieces of the system that will be included and those that will not. Use some method of prioritizing the requirements so you can verify that everything that must be included in the system is there, and you can ensure that things that are not necessary are not worked on.

Some of the requirements you have identified will be obviously necessary—the basic processes of the system. These should be marked some way, such as Required or Must Have. Other requirements are important, but not vital. These could be marked as Important or Should Have. Still others would be nice to have and could be marked as Nice or Could Have. The rest are pie in the sky—something we are dreaming of but probably won't get to this time around. They could be marked as Future or Would Like to Have.

When prioritizing requirements, you also have to consider the risks and market factors you have identified. So Must Haves are not just based on technical necessity, but might also address risks in the marketplace. For National Widgets, this might mean that a Web interface is a Must Have for the order-processing system because every other mail order company offers it. This feature is required just to stay level with the competition.

Choose some way of prioritizing your requirements and use it consistently. Consider a requirements management tool to store this information for later retrieval and report generation.

When scoping your project, you need to estimate what can realistically be accomplished in the time frame allowed, given your budget and resources. All Must Have requirements will have to be included, and most Should Haves. What else can you afford to include?

As you work through the process of defining the boundaries of the system and later as you detail use cases, you may find more requirements for your system. In going through the process you have determined that these requirements are within the boundary of your system. But are they within the scope of your project? Ask yourself these questions:

- Can we afford to add these new requirements on our schedule and budget?
- Should we add a later, second version of the system and address these new requirements then?
- If we have to add them now, can we move other requirements to the later version?

Is This Requirement in Scope?

National Widgets has looked at the market and noticed that Web commerce is really popular. Should they have Web pages, an on-line catalog, and electronic ordering in the first release of the order-processing software? How important is this requirement?

Things that are nice to have but are not required should be considered for a later phase of this system or for a later project. Remember that the hardest part of a project is getting to release 1.0. Going from 1.0 to 1.1 is a lot easier.

CHAPTER REVIEW

At this point you should have a clearly defined boundary for your system as well as a clearly defined scope for your project. Some things to ask yourself are:

- Are the system requirements all represented by use cases? If not, verify that these requirements are internal to your system and can't be seen by the actors. These kinds of requirements don't appear on a use case diagram.
- Do all the actors and use cases have descriptive names? Do those that need further explanation have short descriptions?
- Are the system boundaries and the project scope clearly defined? If not, this becomes a major risk to your project. Clear this up as soon as possible. If questions cannot be answered, make a decision and record it in your list of assumptions.
- Are all areas of uncertainty recorded in the list of assumptions?

Go back and update the project description, risks, assumptions, and so on, as needed to reflect things you have learned while defining the system boundaries.

Table 2-1 shows the deliverables you should have completed. This completes the information gathering for the inception phase. Other activities of

Table 2-1 Inception Phase Deliverables

Complete	Deliverables
✔	Project description
✔	Risk analysis
✔	Use case diagram
✔	Description of actors and use cases
✔	Project proposal

this phase, such as writing a proposal and creating a business justification for the project, are beyond the scope of this book.

Our friends who are starting the mail order company have decided the project is feasible and will go ahead with it. We hope the same is true for your project. We will continue in the next chapter with writing detailed use case descriptions.

Chapter 3

Documenting Use Cases

We have completed the inception phase of our project by deciding that we are going to do this project. It looks feasible to management and marketing. Now we need to spend more time adding details to the technical parts of the documentation.

During the elaboration phase you will spend time adding details to the requirements of the project. You want to finish this phase of the project having confidence that technically it can be completed within a certain time frame and budget. The documents you will be creating include detailed use cases, an architecture, and a project plan. You might also create one or more prototypes to test some particular piece of the system.

THE BASIC USE CASE

Each use case must include details about what has to be done to achieve its functionality. We need to consider the basic functionality, any alternatives, error conditions, anything that must be true before starting the use case, and anything that must be true on exiting the use case. The use case may include conditionals, branching, and loops. Let's look at an example of a possible use case for an order-processing system (see Exhibit 3-1).

The format of this use case works very well for relatively simple use cases. Everything you need to know about the use case is in one place. We can continue refining this, adding branching or alternative flows to show error handling or other alternatives. Let's look at the parts that make up a use case in a little more detail.

Exhibit 3-1 Place Order Use Case

Precondition: A valid user has logged in to the system.

Flow of Events:

1. The use case begins when the customer selects Place Order.

2. The customer enters his or her name and address.

3. If the customer enters only the zip code, the system supplies the city and state.

4. The customer enters product codes for the desired products.

5. The system supplies a product description and price for each item.

6. The system keeps a running total of items ordered as they are entered.

7. The customer enters credit card payment information.

8. The customer selects Submit.

9. The system verifies the information, saves the order as pending, and forwards payment information to the accounting system. If any information is incorrect, the system prompts the customer to correct it.

10. When payment is confirmed, the order is marked confirmed, an order ID is returned to the customer, and the use case ends. If payment is not confirmed, the system will prompt the customer to correct payment information or cancel. If the customer chooses to correct the information, go back to step 7. If the customer chooses to cancel, the use case ends.

Postcondition: If the order was not canceled, it is saved in the system and marked confirmed.

Pre- and Postconditions

Pre- and postconditions indicate what comes before and after the use case. They tell what state the system must be in at the start of the use case (precondition) or what state the system must be in at the end of the use case (postcondition). The postcondition must be true no matter which branch or alternative is followed for the use case.

For an example, we will presume that our order-processing system automatically sends sales tax to the government once every quarter for products sold that quarter. We are simplifying the example by ignoring the fact that sales tax probably will have to be sent to more than one state or locality. We simply want to send in a sales tax payment if it is the end of the quarter. We have to be positive the taxes were credited because the government imposes severe penalties on companies that do not pay their sales tax on time (see Exhibit 3-2).

Exhibit 3-2 Pre- and Postcondition Example in the Deposit Sales Tax Use Case

> **Precondition:** It is the end of one of National Widgets' business quarters.
>
> **Flow of Events:**
>
> 1. The use case begins when the system detects the end of a business quarter.
>
> 2. The system determines the amount of sales tax collected for the quarter.
>
> 3. The system sends an electronic payment of sales tax to the government.
>
> 4. The system verifies the taxes were received and the use case ends.
>
> **Postcondition:** The government has deposited the taxes and updated National Widgets' records.

Note that the postcondition must be true, no matter what. If our electronic payment does not go through for some reason, National Widgets is still responsible for paying the sales tax on time. No matter what errors happen, the postcondition still must be true. This particular postcondition will be complex to verify because the government does not send an acknowledgement that taxes were received.

Flow of Events

The *flow of events* is a series of declarative statements listing the steps of a use case from the actor's point of view. Tell how it begins, using a statement such as "The use case begins when . . ." If the use case is for software, how does the software know when the use case begins? If the use case describes a business process, when does that process start? Similary, how does the use case end? State this explicitly using a phrase such as "The use case ends."

Alternatives can be shown using branching. To show branching, we use an if statement. An example of this is shown in Find Order (see Exhibit 3-3).

Use repetition when you need to repeat a step or a set of steps multiple times. Indicate clearly where the repetition starts and ends. Also indicate clearly how you will end it. It may end because you have gotten to the end of a set of things, or there may be some condition that causes the repetition to stop. Typically we use a for or while to indicate repetition.

We should indicate repetition in our Place Order use case because the user can enter more than one product on a single order. It's implied in the current text, but it is better to make the repetition explicit (see Exhibit 3-4).

Exhibit 3-5 is the same example using while instead of for. They do the same job and look almost identical in text. Use whichever is easier for you and your team to read and understand.

Exhibit 3-3 Branching Example in the Find Order Use Case

Flow of Events:

1. The use case begins when the user chooses Find an Order.

2. The user may enter an order ID, customer ID, or customer name.

3. The user presses Find.

4. If the user entered an order ID

    a) The system displays that order and the use case ends.

5. If the user entered a customer name or customer ID

    a) The system returns a list of all orders for that customer.

    b) The user selects one order from the list.

    c) The system displays that order and the use case ends.

Exhibit 3-4 Repetition Example with for in the Place Order Use Case

---

Flow of Events:

1. The use case begins when the customer selects Place Order.

2. The customer enters his or her name and address.

3. If the customer enters only the zip code, the system supplies the city and state.

4. The customer enters product codes for products to be ordered.

5. For each product code entered

    a) the system supplies a product description and price.

    b) the system adds the price of the item to the total.

end loop

6. The customer enters credit card payment information.

7. The customer selects Submit.

8. The system verifies the information, saves the order as pending, and forwards payment information to the accounting system. If any information is incorrect, the system prompts the customer to correct it.

9. When payment is confirmed, the order is marked confirmed, an order ID is returned to the customer, and the use case ends. If payment is not confirmed, the system will prompt the customer to correct payment information or cancel. If the customer chooses to correct the information, go back to step 6 in the Basic Path. If the customer chooses to cancel, the use case ends.

Exhibit 3-5 Repetition Example with `while` in the Place Order Use Case

Flow of Events:

1. The use case begins when the customer selects Place Order.

2. The customer enters his or her name and address.

3. If the customer enters only the zip code, the system supplies the city and state.

4. While the customer enters product codes

    a) The system supplies a product description and price.

    b) The system adds the price of the item to the total.

end loop

5. The customer enters credit card payment information.

6. The customer selects Submit.

7. The system verifies the information, saves the order as pending, and forwards payment information to the accounting system. If any information is incorrect, the system prompts the customer to correct it.

8. When payment is confirmed, the order is marked confirmed, an order ID is returned to the customer, and the use case ends. If payment is not confirmed, the system will prompt the customer to correct payment information or cancel. If the customer chooses to correct the information, go back to step 5 in the Basic Path. If the customer chooses to cancel, the use case ends.

GUIDELINES FOR CORRECTNESS AND COMPLETENESS

Now is a good time to review the use cases you have written. Chapter 8 has quite a bit of information on different kinds of reviews. In this section we have included some simple things to consider when first reviewing your use cases.

Each step of the use case should be a simple declarative statement. By default the steps will be in order by time. What if the steps can happen in any order? If this is the case, make it clear in the description. This could be a simple statement at the beginning of the use case that the steps can run concurrently. Or you might state that some of the steps can happen in any order.

Resist the temptation to get too detailed. We will add more detail over time. But at this point in the process, we are collecting requirements, not doing detailed analysis or design. On the other hand, the use case needs to be complete. Be very clear on the start and end points, and make sure the list of steps covers in general everything you need to accomplish the functionality of the use case.

You will find a large percentage of use cases start and end with an actor. From our order-processing system, we see that Place Order starts and ends with the customer. Some smaller number of use cases start with an actor and end internally or start inside the system and end with an actor. We have found this convenient when dealing with time. For example, if our order-processing system is automated to check once a week and place an order for back-ordered items from a supplier, this would start internally and end with the supplier actor.

By definition, use cases are written from the actor's point of view. Therefore, all the steps in your use cases should be visible to or easily surmised by the actor.

Use cases are a communication tool. They are effective only when they communicate information about how the system works to the reader. It is important to consider who will be reading the use cases. Will it be end users, marketing specialists, developers, or management? Whoever it is, they have to be able to understand the use cases. If they don't, then the use cases need to be rewritten.

Another correctness check is to look at each step of the basic path one by one. For each step ask yourself, "What is the most likely thing to occur here?" That is what should be written for that particular step.

Don't worry about getting the use cases perfect. The nature of the process is to be iterative; you keep looking back over work you have already done and refine it to reflect knowledge learned. The use cases will improve as your understanding of the system improves.

On the other hand, you must include enough information in the use cases to be able to determine whether a particular use case handles a particular functionality.

If you show an actor communicating with a use case in a diagram, then that actor must be referenced somewhere in the use case. Where does that communication take place?

PRESENTATION STYLES

Use cases can be written very formally or in a less formal style. Keep in mind who will be reading the use cases and choose a style that is comfortable for the readers. Potential readers of use cases include end users, customers, marketing specialists, customer advisory boards, users groups, testers, technical writers, system architects, system engineers, several levels of management, and developers.

A use case could be written as informal text (see Exhibit 3-6). Or it could be a numbered list of steps (see Exhibit 3-7). Or it could be in a table format (see Exhibit 3-8). Choose a style that is best for your intended audience. Our experience is that, in general, a numbered list is easier to understand across a

Exhibit 3-6 Informal Text Form of the Cancel Order Use Case

When the customer rep receives a request to cancel an order, the customer rep finds the order in the system and marks it canceled. Then a request is sent to the accounting system to credit the customer's account.

Exhibit 3-7 Numbered Steps Form of the Cancel Order Use Case

1. The use case begins when the customer rep receives a request to cancel an order.
2. The customer rep enters an order ID.
3. The customer rep presses Find.
4. The system displays that order.
5. The customer rep chooses Cancel.
6. The system marks the order canceled.
7. The accounting system is notified to credit the customer's account and the use case ends.

Exhibit 3-8 Table Form of the Cancel Order Use Case

Customer Rep	System	Accounting System
1. Receives a request to cancel an order		
2. Enters an order ID		
3. Presses Find		
	4. Displays the order	
5. Chooses Cancel		
	6. Marks the order canceled	
		7. Credits the customer's account.

wider range of audience types. It shows each step distinctly, steps can be referred to by number in discussions, and it is an easy style to read for most audiences.

OTHER REQUIREMENTS

As you write each use case, you may find some requirements for your system that are not visible to the actors. Or you may have some special requirements that are hard to express in use cases. These could be things such as timing and size requirements for real time systems. Or for our order-processing software, we have a requirement to provide fast, efficient service, which doesn't turn into a use case. Instead, it affects a lot of other use cases.

These other requirements need to be written and kept with your use cases. They also are a part of your system. They are things that will have to be included as you build and test the system. You can include them in another requirements document that is kept with the use cases documents. Like the use cases, these requirements can be prioritized and managed by a require-ments management tool.

Sometimes these requirements are referred to as non-functional require-ments. These include things such as usability, security, the need for persistent data, maintainability, performance, load, or the need to be fail-safe.

If the requirements are specific to a particular use case, you can add a spe-cial requirements section to the use case description (see Exhibit 3-9). For example, we will require the Place Order use case to respond to any user input within one second.

Other documents are frequently developed along with the use cases. These include a glossary of terms, a data definition document describing the format and validation rules for data elements, and guidelines for the user interface. We look at these documents in more detail in Chapter 7. You may also want to maintain a document that lists outstanding issues or questions that need to be addressed.

HANDLING COMPLEX USE CASES

The Place Order use case is relatively detailed but is still not complete. We haven't considered all possible error conditions, for example, nor have we really detailed the interaction with the customer or customer rep. The system may behave somewhat differently for each of these actors. What about access control and logon permissions? This is a relatively simple use case. How can we handle the more complex use cases?

Exhibit 3-9 Special Requirements in Place Order

Flow of Events:

1. The use case begins when the customer selects Place Order.

2. The customer enters his or her name and address.

3. If the customer enters only the zip code, the system supplies the city and state.

4. While the customer enters product codes
   a) the system supplies a product description and price.
   b) the system adds the price of the item to the total.

end loop

5. The customer enters credit card payment information.

6. The customer selects Submit.

7. The system verifies the information, saves the order as pending, and forwards payment information to the accounting system. If any information is incorrect, the system prompts the customer to correct it.

8. When payment is confirmed, the order is marked confirmed, an order ID is returned to the customer, and the use case ends. If payment is not confirmed, the system will prompt the customer to correct payment information or cancel. If the customer chooses to correct the information, go back to step 5 in the Basic Path. If the customer chooses to cancel, the use case ends.

Special Requirements:

The system must always respond to user input within one second.

A complete use case description can get quite complicated. This is not something you write at the very beginning. This is a description that evolves over time. We document the use case flow of events in several sections to make it easier to read. The sections can be written one at a time until the use case is complete.

The flow of events is divided into two sections: the basic path and the alternative paths. We will start writing the basic path by choosing the most common sequence of steps for the use case. After writing the basic path, we can add alternatives and exceptions to the use case. These are the alternative paths of the use case.

THE BASIC PATH

 The basic path is written as if everything goes right. There are no bugs, no errors; it is a perfect world. It is often called the happy day scenario. There must be one basic path for each use case.

Write the basic path just as we have been writing the flow of events. The difference is that the basic path is a series of simple declarative statements with no branching or alternatives. You won't have if statements in the basic path. At each step, assume everything is correct. Pick the most common way of doing each step.

As you go through this process, you may find new use cases or actors for your system, or new risk factors for the project. Update all your documents to reflect what you learn as you write the scenarios.

"Hi," Gus murmured as he sat down. "Sorry I'm late. I got stuck at work. Where are we?"

"We're looking over the actors for anything we've missed. If you're hungry, Dennis made us save some of his barbecue specialties for you."

"Great! I am starved! Okay, you fill me in while I grab some of that delicious-looking food."

"Well," Tara said, "we were just deciding that we had found all of our actors and use cases, but we don't know where to go next. We can't figure out how to turn all this stuff into something useful. They show us *what* they work with but not how to turn that information into something we need. For example, how does an order get to shipping?"

"Well, that's what we have to do next. Have you got your list of actors? Good! This is where we put our actors to work and see how the system flows. What we want to do is take each action an actor can do and follow it through our system, one step at a time. Let's look at a customer entering an order." (See Exhibit 3-10.)

"Okay," Lisa told Dennis. "We have Customer Places Order written down. But when do we deposit the money? Do we deposit it when the customer orders or after we ship? And what happens if it's a check, not a credit card payment?"

"But I'd hate to charge someone when they order it. What happens if we have to back-order something? They've already paid for it!"

"Hey! Wait a minute!" Gus demanded. "I said we just wanted to write down the happy-day scenario. We only want to find the ones where everything goes right. We'll worry about the ones that don't later on, so don't get bogged down on all the variations. Let's go on with the other major things that can happen."

"Well," Dennis said, "this basic path is really useful. So far, we've found out that we need Place Order to talk to the accounting system, and since Place Order needs a product description and price, it probably also talks to the inventory system."

"Does that mean we have to go back and add it to our use case diagram?"

"Of course! That's exactly what it means. Remember, the diagram was just what we knew about the process at the exact time we wrote it down. Now that we have learned more about it, we go back and change it. This way, it grows along with our knowledge."

Exhibit 3-10 Place Order Basic Path

Flow of Events:

Basic Path

1. The use case begins when the customer selects Place Order.

2. The customer enters his or her name and address.

3. While the customer enters product codes

    a) The system supplies a product description and price.

    b) The system adds the price of the item to the total.

end loop

4. The customer enters credit card payment information.

5. The customer selects Submit.

6. The system verifies the information, saves the order as pending, and forwards payment information to the accounting system.

7. When payment is confirmed, the order is marked confirmed, an order ID is returned to the customer, and the use case ends.

"Hey, does that mean we have to go back and look at everything else we've done? Like the list of risks, use case diagrams, and so on?"

"Very good, Tara! Yes, it does. As we learn more about our system, we update all documentation to match what we learned. Let's finish writing a basic path for each use case, then go back and update our diagrams to match what we learn."

"Well," Gus said, "this diagram [Exhibit 3-11] is getting rather messy. There are some techniques for cleaning it up. But let's review our use cases first, then come back to this diagram and clean it up."

ALTERNATIVE PATHS

An alternative path is one that allows a different sequence of events than what was used for the basic path. Maybe a user can pick one of several things to do at some point in the use case. The most likely choice was documented in the basic path. Now we document the rest of the choices as alternative paths.

We also document errors as alternative paths. What can go wrong and what will we do about it? What if a transaction is canceled in the middle? What do we do in that situation?

Alternative paths are particularly good for showing things that can happen at any time, such as canceling a transaction or accessing context-specific

Exhibit 3-11 Order-Processing Use Cases

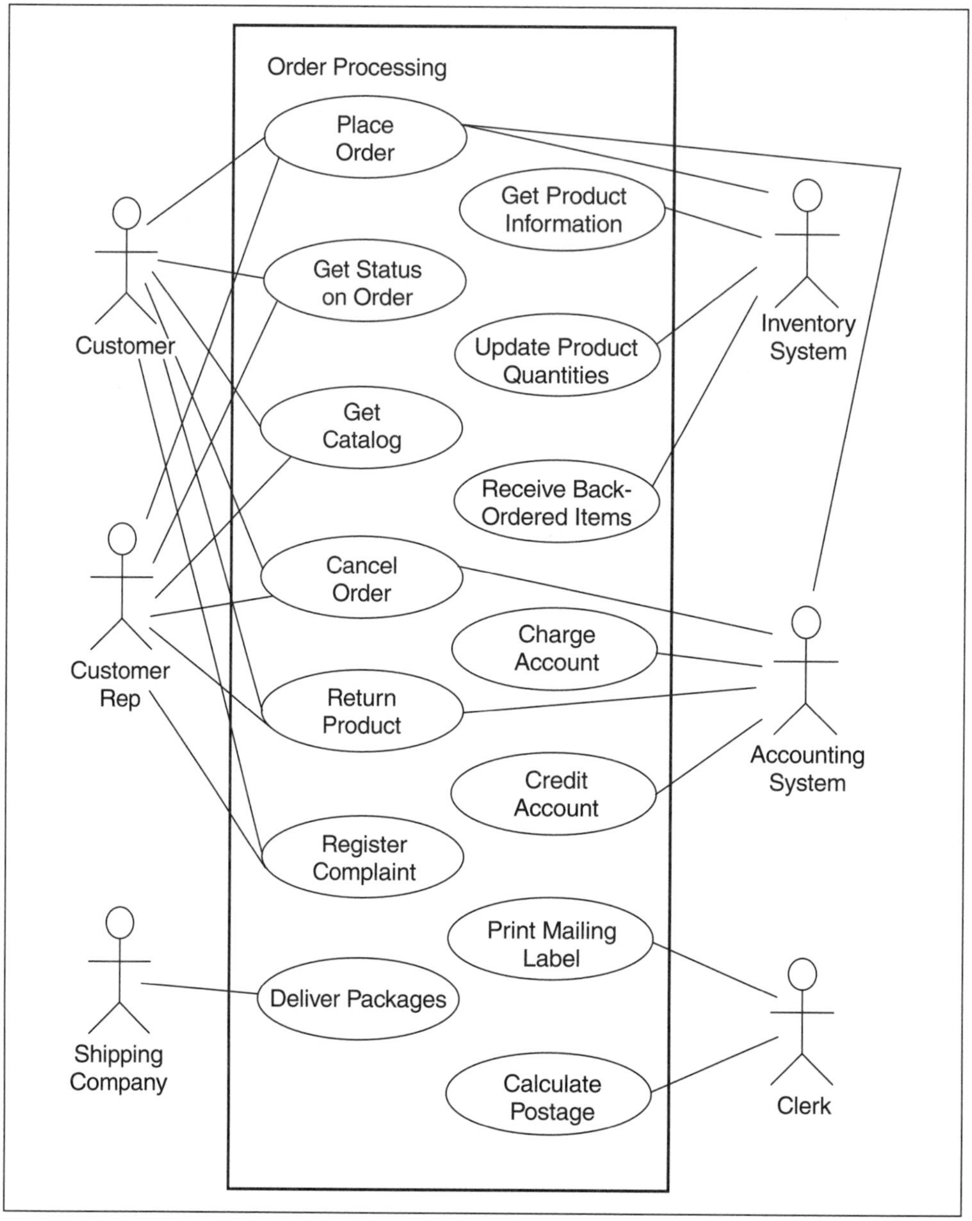

help. For example, during the Place Order use case, the customer can cancel the order at any time before it is submitted (see Exhibit 3-12).

When the use case is executing, if the user selects Cancel, we jump to the alternative flow of events and execute it. This technique can be applied to exception handling as well as interrupt handling in use cases.

Exhibit 3-12 Alternative Paths Example in the Place Order Use Case

---

Flow of Events:

Basic Path

1. The use case begins when the customer selects Place Order.

2. The customer enters his or her name and address.

3. While the customer enters product codes

    a) The system supplies a product description and price.

    b) The system adds the price of the item to the total.

end loop

4. The customer enters credit card payment information.

5. The customer selects Submit.

6. The system verifies the information, saves the order as pending, and forwards payment information to the accounting system.

7. When payment is confirmed, the order is marked confirmed, an order ID is returned to the customer, and the use case ends.

Alternative Paths

- At any time before selecting submit, the customer can select Cancel. The order is not saved and the use case ends.

- In step 6, if any information is incorrect, the system prompts the customer to correct the information.

- In step 7, if payment is not confirmed, the system prompts the customer to correct payment information or cancel. If the customer chooses to correct the information, go back to step 4 in the Basic Path. If the customer chooses to cancel, the use case ends.

"Okay, Gus," Tara said. "We've got a basic path for each and every use case that we wrote up. I think I see how this is starting to help us! Now what?"

"Well, now we keep going. Remember back a while ago, when you tried to write down a use case where things went wrong? I stopped you then because we wanted to focus on getting down the major pieces. Now that we have them, we go back and fill them out. That is to say, we start with, oh, Customer Places Order. Then we follow it through one step at a time. At each step, we think of all the things that can go wrong."

"Wow!" Lisa exclaimed. "That could be quite a list!"

"Well, we don't want to write down *all* of the possibilities in detail or we'd end up doing our entire project in English. We want to write down representative actions. For example, if we are doing a scenario where the deposited money from a customer order doesn't go into our account. What could be the reasons? Well, they could have closed the account, there could have been insufficient funds, or any number of other reasons. But the main focus for us would be that it didn't go into our account. That's the only one we would document."

"Okay, that sounds a little better. How should we find these? And how do we write them down?"

"One way is to take one basic path and then, line by line, ask what can go wrong or what can be done differently. Each time you get a different answer, it's a new alternative path. Let's start writing and see what we end up with."

One method for finding alternative paths is to go through the basic path line by line and ask questions:

- Is there some other action that can be taken at this point?
- Is there something that can go wrong at this point?
- Is there some behavior that can happen at any time?

Another method is to use categories to discover alternatives. Some examples follow:

- An actor exits the application.
- An actor cancels a particular operation.
- An actor requests help.
- An actor provides bad data.
- An actor provides incomplete data.
- An actor chooses an alternative way of performing the use case.
- The system crashes.
- The system is unavailable.

Each alternative path needs a name and/or a brief description (see Exhibit 3-13).

That's all you will do for now. For each basic path, simply list all the alternatives and exceptions you can think of. As you identify the alternatives and exceptions, update the list of assumptions with any new assumptions you find. The list will be included in the documentation that is reviewed by customers, marketing, users, or whoever is defining your project.

DETAILING SIGNIFICANT BEHAVIOR

Alternative paths that are important or complex also will need a sequence of steps detailing their behavior. You can write them the same way you write the basic path. Pick a readable style, check for completeness and correctness, and keep your writing style consistent with the primary scenarios.

Exhibit 3-13 Place Order Additional Alternative Paths by Category

---

Incomplete Data

Payment not there
Order incomplete
Shipping address is incomplete

Bad Data

Customer can't log in due to bad password or username
Product code doesn't match actual products
Product no longer carried
Payment bad

Alternative Behavior

Customer pays by check
Customer sends order by mail
Customer phones in order

Actor Cancels Operation

Customer cancels placing the order

System Crash

The system crashes partway through placing the order

System Unavailable

Customer can't log in due to system not responding
Order gets lost

"Well," Lisa said, putting down her pen, "I think I'm getting the hang of this. We're just putting names down, not the detailed list of steps like before."

"Right. But some of these we will pick out and write up a detailed list of steps."

"How do we pick the ones to detail?" Tara asked.

"Look for alternatives that look like they would be complex or ones you think could be important. We can look over our risk list and pick out alternatives that address those risks. They would be good choices for detailing."

"Hey, Gus!" Dennis said. "How about this one? Payment Bad. That's sure important to me, because I'll go out of business if I don't get paid."

"Sure. Let's look for some more."

DOCUMENTING ALTERNATIVES

We have seen a couple of ways to document alternatives in a use case. In this section, we'll use the Place Order use case basic path, modify it in various ways to show the techniques together, and discuss advantages and disadvantages of each technique (see Exhibit 3-14).

One technique is to add the alternatives directly to the text of the use case, adding new numbered steps as appropriate. The advantage is that it is very easy to see all possible behavior for this use case. The disadvantage of this approach is that it tends to make the use case hard to read and understand. Also, if you are using the step numbers to identify requirements, you won't want to change step numbers to add alternative paths later (see Exhibit 3-15).

Another technique is to add the alternatives in paragraphs under the original steps. This tends to be easier to read than the previous example. The original steps become an outline to the basic path of the use case, and the details of alternatives and error handling are in the paragraphs below the numbered steps. There is no change to the original step numbering (see Exhibit 3-16).

A third technique is to put the alternatives in a different section of the use case document, called the alternative paths section. This section of the document follows the basic path. The advantages to this approach are that the basic path is easy to read, and there is plenty of room to show details to the

Exhibit 3-14 Original Place Order Use Case

Flow of Events:

Basic Path

1. The use case begins when the customer selects Place Order.

2. The customer enters his or her name and address.

3. While the customer enters product codes

    a) the system supplies a product description and price.

    b) the system adds the price of the item to the total.

end loop

4. The customer enters credit card payment information.

5. The customer selects Submit.

6. The system verifies the information, saves the order as pending, and forwards payment information to the accounting system.

7. When payment is confirmed, the order is marked confirmed, an order ID is returned to the customer, and the use case ends.

Exhibit 3-15 Place Order Use Case with Alternatives in Text

Flow of Events:

Basic Path

1. The use case begins when the customer selects Place Order.

2. The customer enters his or her name and address.

3. If the customer enters only the zip code, the system supplies the city and state.

4. The customer enters product codes for products to be ordered.

5. For each product code entered

   a) If the product code is in the system, the system supplies a product description and price, and adds the price of the item to the total.

   b) If the product code is not in the system, the system prints an error message and prompts the customer to enter a new product code.

end loop

6. The customer enters credit card payment information.

7. The customer selects Submit.

8. The system verifies the payment information.

9. If all information is correct, the use case continues with step 13.

10. If the customer did not enter payment information, the system prompts the customer to enter the information or cancel.

11. If the customer chooses to cancel, the use case ends.

12. If the customer enters new payment information, the customer selects submit, and the use case repeats from step 8.

13. The system saves the order as pending, and forwards payment information to the accounting system.

14. If the accounting system confirms the payment is good, the order is marked confirmed, an order ID is returned to the customer, and the use case ends.

15. If the accounting system returns an error, the system prints an error message and prompts the customer to enter new payment information or cancel.

16. If the customer chooses cancel, the use case ends.

17. If the customer chooses to enter new payment information, the use case repeats from step 6.

Exhibit 3-16   Place Order Use Case with Alternatives in Paragraphs

---

Flow of Events:

Basic Path

1. The use case begins when the customer selects Place Order.

2. The customer enters his or her name and address.

If the customer enters only the zip code, the system supplies the city and state.

3. The customer enters product codes for products to be ordered.

4. For each product code entered

   a) the system supplies a product description and price.

If the product code is not in the system, the system displays an error message and prompts the customer to enter a new product code.

   b) the system adds the price of the item to the total.

 The system does not change the total for items not found in the system.

end loop

5. The customer enters credit card payment information.

6. The customer selects Submit.

7. The system verifies the information, saves the order as pending, and forwards payment information to the accounting system.

If the customer did not enter payment infomation, the system prompts the customer to enter the information or cancel. If the customer chooses to cancel, the use case ends. If the customer enters new payment information, the customer selects submit, and the use case repeats from step 7.

8. When payment is confirmed, the order is marked confirmed, an order ID is returned to the customer, and the use case ends.

If the accounting system returns an error, the system prints an error message and prompts the customer to enter new payment information or cancel. If the customer chooses cancel, the use case ends. If the customer chooses to enter new payment information, the use case repeats from step 5.

---

alternatives. Some people don't like this because finding all the information about an alternative might mean having to look through several pages of document (see Exhibit 3-17).

    The alternative paths can be written in a paragraph format, as shown in Exhibit 3-17, or you may choose to write them out in the same style as the basic path (see Exhibit 3-18).

Exhibit 3-17   Place Order Use Case with an Alternative Paths Section

---

Flow of Events:

Basic Path

1. The use case begins when the customer selects Place Order.

2. The customer enters his or her name and address.

3. The customer enters product codes for products to be ordered.

4. For each product code entered
   a) The system supplies a product description and price.
   b) The system adds the price of the item to the total.

end loop

5. The customer enters credit card payment information.

6. The customer selects Submit.

7. The system verifies the information, saves the order as pending, and forwards payment information to the accounting system.

8. When payment is confirmed, the order is marked confirmed, an order ID is returned to the customer, and the use case ends.

Alternative Paths

- In step 7, if any information is incorrect, the system prompts the customer to correct the information.

- At any time before selecting submit, the customer can cancel the order and the use case ends.

- In step 8, if payment is not confirmed, the system prompts the customer to correct payment information or cancel. If the customer chooses to correct the information, go back to step 5 in the Basic Path. If the customer chooses to cancel, the use case ends.

Exhibit 3-18   Place Order Use Case Detailed Alternative Paths Section

---

Alternative Paths

Alternative 1: Incorrect data

1. This alternative begins in step 7 of the basic path when the system detects incorrect information.

2. The system prompts the customer to correct the information.

3. The basic path continues with step 7.

Alternative 2: Cancel

1. At any time in the Place Order use case, the customer may select cancel.

2. The system prompts the customer to verify the cancel.

3. The customer selects OK and the use case ends.

The method of documentation you choose will depend on the complexity of the use case. Simpler use cases can be documented with the alternatives in place. More complex use cases will be easier to read if alternatives are written separately. We frequently combine approaches, putting simple alternatives in the basic path and more complex alternatives in the alternative paths section (see Exhibit 3-19).

Exhibit 3-19 Place Order Use Case with an Alternative Paths Section

---

Flow of Events:

Basic Path

1. The use case begins when the customer selects Place Order.

2. The customer enters his or her name and address.

3. If the customer enters only the zip code, the system supplies the city and state.

4. The customer enters product codes for products to be ordered.

5. For each product code entered

    a) the system supplies a product description and price.

    b) the system adds the price of the item to the total.

end loop

6. The customer enters credit card payment information.

7. The customer selects Submit.

8. The system verifies the information, saves the order as pending, and forwards payment information to the accounting system.

9. When payment is confirmed, the order is marked confirmed, an order ID is returned to the customer, and the use case ends.

Alternative Paths

Alternative 1: Incorrect data

1. This alternative begins in step 8 of the basic path when the system detects incorrect information.

2. The system prompts the customer to correct the information.

3. The basic path continues with step 8.

Alternative 2: Cancel

1. At any time in the Place Order use case, the customer may select cancel.

2. The system prompts the customer to verify the cancel.

3. The customer selects OK and the use case ends.

How detailed should the alternatives be? You can write out a complete sequence of steps for every alternative path, but this is unnecessarily time-consuming. In many cases alternative paths will vary from the basic path and from one another by a very small amount. Instead of writing out a whole sequence of steps, just note the variation in your brief description of the alternative. Writing a complete set of detailed descriptions takes time that could be put to better use building your system. There is no point in building your whole system in a natural language, such as English. There are no automatic English-to-Java translators!

SCENARIOS

If you pick one particular path through the use case, that is called a scenario. For the Place Order use case just described, some of the scenarios include:

- An order arrives that is complete, with the correct payment.
- An order arrives that is missing a payment.
- An order arrives that is missing a shipping address.

Each of these scenarios describes one path through the Place Order use case. If you combine all the scenarios for Place Order, you get the complete use case. Each scenario represents one instance of the use case.

ADDING DIRECTION TO THE COMMUNICATES ASSOCIATION

Until now we have not been concerned with the direction of the communicates association. Now that we have written the details of the use cases, we know who initiates the use case—an actor, the system, or both. The direction of initiation is shown by adding an arrowhead to the communicates association.

Let's look at a couple of examples. The Place Order use case is clearly started by the customer actor. We update the use case diagram to add an arrow from the customer to Place Order (see Exhibit 3-20).

Exhibit 3-20 Place Order Use Case Initiated by Customer Actor

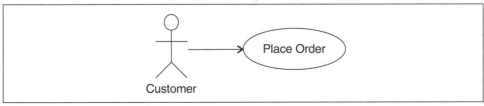

The Get Status on Order use case is less clear. We could have the customer always request status (see Exhibit 3-21) or have the system send a message to the customer when status changes (see Exhibit 3-22) or both (see Exhibit 3-23). We do not put two arrowheads on the same line, but use separate arrows to make it explicit that the use case can be initiated both directions.

CHAPTER REVIEW

In this chapter, we have looked at the basic form of a use case, which includes precondition, flow of events, and postcondition. We created the first flow of events for each use case by writing one basic path. Then we reviewed it for correctness and completeness. We added alternative paths to the use case, choosing a documentation style appropriate to our project. We also considered different styles for writing use cases, each appropriate for a different

Exhibit 3-21   Get Status on Order Use Case Initiated by Customer Actor

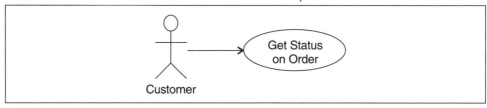

Exhibit 3-22   Get Status on Order Use Case Initiated by the System

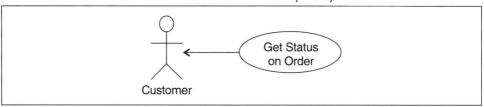

Exhibit 3-23   Get Status on Order Use Case Initiated by Customer Actor or the System

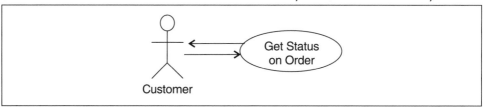

kind of audience. The next chapter considers advanced techniques for organizing use cases.

Table 3-1 shows the deliverables that should be complete.

Table 3-1 Elaboration Phase Deliverables

Complete	Deliverables
✔	Detailed basic path
✔	Alternative paths
	Activity diagrams
	User interface diagrammed (optional)
	Architecture
	Project plan

Chapter 4

Advanced Use Case Documentation Techniques

As you continue refining the flows of events, you may find similarity in the various use cases that you want to abstract into a common place. Or you may want to extend a use case without changing the original description. You also may find a lot of similarities in some of the actors. To take advantage of these similarities in your system, you can apply some techniques.

Do not sacrifice clarity for convenience, however. Your goal always should be to produce a clear, easy-to-understand document. For that reason, the only one of the following techniques that we apply to documents for end users is include. The other techniques—extend, interfaces, and inheritance—are really of interest to development staff, not end users.

INCLUDE

If you find yourself cutting and pasting the same block of text over and over, it indicates you have something generic you can reuse. You can abstract the common behavior with an include relationship. Start out by identifying the steps that you want to use in many places. Put the steps in a use case and give them a name.

For example, in our order-processing system we need a set of steps to search for an order by customer ID, order ID, or customer name. This searching is done from many of the use cases, including Get Status on Order, Cancel Order, Return Product, and so on. We'll call this use case Find Order (see Exhibit 4-1). Now, remove these steps from the original use cases and replace them with a reference to the new use case (see Exhibit 4-2).

When the Cancel Order use case reaches the Include Find Order step, it executes the steps of Find Order, then returns to Cancel Order and continues with the next step. We show this relationship on a use case diagram (see Exhibit 4-3).

Note that the Including use case is no longer complete by itself. It must have the use cases it is including to be complete. On the other hand, the use

Exhibit 4-1   Find Order Use Case

1. The use case begins when the customer enters an order ID, customer ID, or customer name.

2. The customer clicks on Find.

3. If the customer entered an order ID
   a) The system displays that order and the use case ends.

4. If the customer entered a customer name or customer ID
   a) The system returns a list of all orders for that customer.
   b) The customer selects one order from the list.
   c) The system displays that order and the use case ends.

Exhibit 4-2   Cancel Order Use Case with an Include Relationship

1. The use case begins when the customer requests to cancel an order.

2. Include Find Order.

3. If the order status is confirmed
   a) The system marks the order canceled.
   b) The system notifies the accounting system to credit the customer's account and the use case ends.

4. If the order status is shipped
   a) The system notifies the customer of National Widgets' return policy and the use case ends.

Exhibit 4-3   Cancel Order Diagram with Included Use Case

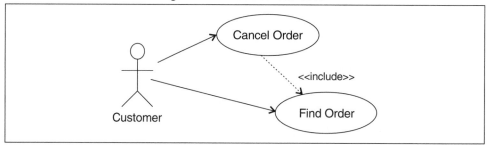

case being included does not know when or if it is being included. Therefore, it cannot have dependencies on any use case that is including it. In our example in Exhibit 4-3, Cancel Order is not a complete use case. It must have Find Order to be complete. But, Find Order does not know that it is being included by Cancel Order.

In Exhibit 4-3 we show an arrow from the customer to Find Order. This arrow is not part of the include relationship. This extra arrow indicates that Find Order is a complete use case that the customer can access independent of Cancel Order.

A use case can include any number of other use cases. You can have as many levels of including as you desire. From our example, Find Order itself can include other use cases. Or, Cancel Order could be included by other use cases.

EXTEND

Extend is used to conditionally extend the behavior of an existing use case. It's a way of adding behavior to a use case without changing the original use case. We typically use extend when working on a later version of an existing product or to indicate places where a product can be customized.

Start by determining what you want to add to the use case and where in the use case it should be added. For example, let's say after working with the order-processing system for a while, National Widgets calls us and says we need to add the ability to offer special discounts to frequent customers and to offer sales on selected merchandise at various times. We identify the Place Order use case as the place where we need to add the new behavior. We don't want to change the original use case because we want to be able to reuse it in another application. So we'll add an extension point after getting the price for an item to allow applying a sale price to that item. We'll also add an extension point after getting the order total so we can apply a special customer discount to the whole order.

Now, we update the use case diagram to include extension points. An extension point labels a place in the use case where extension is allowed. The use case is not required to be extended, but if it is, the extension points indicate where the extension(s) may occur. Each extension point has a unique name and a description of a location in the use case. These extension points are shown on the use case diagram by adding an extension point compartment to the use case oval (see Exhibit 4-4). Notice that we did not change the use case description. The use case being extended does not change (see Exhibit 4-5).

Exhibit 4-4 Place Order Use Case with Extension Points

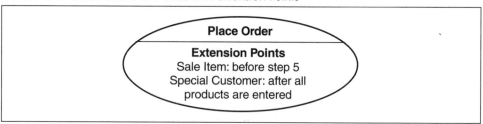

Exhibit 4-5 Place Order Use Case

1. The use case begins when the customer selects Place Order.

2. The customer enters his or her name and address.

3. The customer enters product codes for the products to be ordered.

4. For each product code entered

   a) The system supplies a product description and price.

   b) The system adds the price of the item to the total.

end loop

5. The customer enters credit card payment information.

6. The customer selects Submit.

7. The system verifies the information, saves the order as pending, and forwards payment information to the accounting system.

8. When payment is confirmed, the order is marked confirmed, an order ID is returned to the customer, and the use case ends.

Finally, we write a use case describing what will happen at the extension point (see Exhibits 4-6 and 4-7) and determine the condition under which the use case will be extended. When the extension point is reached, if the condition is true, the steps in the extension are executed. The condition is shown in the use case diagram along with the extension point being used. The condition and extension point are part of the relationship, not part of the use case. The relationship between the use case and its extensions is shown in Exhibit 4-8.

Note that our extended use case—Place Order—must work whether or not it is extended. It cannot know that it has been extended. Extension is allowed but may never take place. In fact, version 1.0 of our product did not include sale items or special customers. National Widgets asked for those fea-

Exhibit 4-6 Extending Use Case Seasonal Sale Price

Basic Path

1. The use case begins when the system gets the sale discount for the product.

2. The system displays the discount on the order.

3. The system calculates a discount amount by multiplying the original price by the sale discount.

4. The system subtracts the discount amount from the order total and the use case ends.

Exhibit 4-7 Extending Use Case Frequent Customer Discount

Basic Path

1. The use case begins when the system gets the customer discount.

2. The system displays the discount on the order.

3. The system calculates a discount amount by multiplying the order total by the customer discount.

4. The system subtracts the discount amount from the order total and the use case ends.

Exhibit 4-8 Place Order Diagram with Extending Use Cases

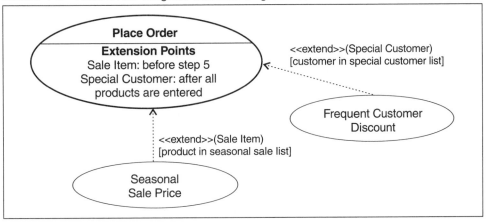

tures to be added later. Even after adding these features we could choose to never have sales or offer special discounts.

So, how does the extension work in our example? If we have a sale, we do the Place Order use case as usual, but at the extension point we add the steps from Seasonal Sale Price. Then we continue with the steps of Place Order. If we don't have a sale, we do not execute the extension.

More than one use case can extend from the same point. More than one extension can be executed for the same extension point. When the extension point is reached, the conditions in all the extending use cases for that point are evaluated. Every extension with a true condition is executed. The order of execution of the extending use cases is undefined.

For example, let's add another extending use case for the sale item extension point (see Exhibit 4-9). If an item is on a seasonal sale and it is overstocked, both of these extending use cases will be executed at the sale item extension point. We update the use case diagram (see Exhibit 4-10) to include this additional extending use case.

Exhibit 4-9 Extending Use Case Overstock Product Sale

1. The use case begins when the system gets the overstock discount for the product.

2. They system displays the discount on the order.

3. The system calculates a discount amount by multiplying the original price by the overstock discount.

4. The system subtracts the discount amount from the order total and the use case ends.

Exhibit 4-10 Place Order Diagram with Extending Use Cases

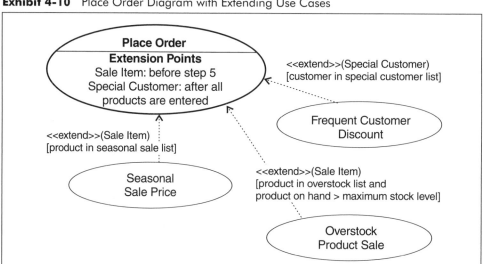

The extending use case may include steps for more than one extension point in the use case. The conditional expression is evaluated once when the first extension point is reached. If it is true, then all the steps in the extending use case are inserted at the appropriate extension points. The extend relationship in the use case diagram will include all the appropriate extension points in an ordered list.

Say, for example, we want to add debugging to our Place Order use case. We want to do something at every extension point in Place Order if debugging is turned on. We can do this with one extending use case (see Exhibit 4-11). If debugging is turned on, the segments of this use case will be inserted into Place Order; the first segment at the first extension point, the second segment at the next extension point, and so on through the list of extension points. We also update the use case diagram to show the debugging use case (see Exhibit 4-12).

Exhibit 4-11   Extending Use Case Debugging

Segment

1. Print "We checked for sale items"

Segment

1. Print "We checked for special customers"

Exhibit 4-12   Place Order Diagram with Multiple Extensions in One Use Case

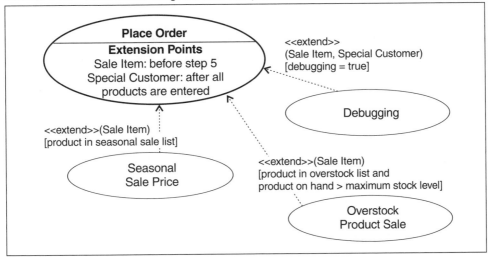

INHERITANCE

In the use case diagram, inheritance can be used between actors or use cases. Inheritance is a "kind-of" relationship, where one element is a kind of the other element. Inheritance between actors means that one actor fills the same roles as another actor. It also may fill additional roles. It interacts with the same uses cases in the same way. Inheritance between use cases means one use case is a specialized version of another use case. The specialized use case inherits behavior from the general use case and may add to it. In the UML, inheritance is indicated by a generalization relationship.

Let's look at a simple example from the order-processing system. Customer and Customer Rep have the same set of use cases they interact with. We can clean up the diagram a lot by putting inheritance between these actors. We'll present only a couple of the use cases for now to show the notation (see Exhibit 4-13).

In this example, Customer interacts with Place Order and Get Status on Order. Customer Rep also interacts with Place Order and Get Status on Order. Because it inherits from Customer, it inherits all the relationships Customer has to these use cases. In addition, Customer Rep interacts with the use case Run Sales Report. The customer is not allowed to do this.

Similarly for the use cases, we have added two new ones, Place Web Order and Place Telephone Order, which inherit from Place Order. These use cases can be documented basically in two ways. First, Place Order itself may be just a description. Place Web Order and Place Telephone Order will have detailed flows of events (see Exhibits 4-14 through 4-16).

Exhibit 4-13 Example of Inheritance in a Use Case Diagram

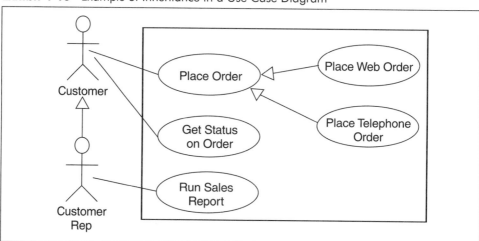

Exhibit 4-14   Place Order Use Case

This use case allows a customer to place orders for products from National Widgets. The data required for this use case includes the customer's billing address, payment information, and a list of products ordered. Optionally, the customer can specify a shipping address different from the billing address.

Exhibit 4-15   Place Telephone Order Use Case

1. The use case begins when the customer calls a customer service representative at National Widgets.

2. The customer service representative gets a catalog ID from the customer and enters it into the system.

3. The system gets the customer name and address from the database.

4. The customer service representative verifies that information with the customer.

5. The customer service representative gets product codes from the customer and enters them into the system.

6. For each product code entered

   a) The system supplies a product description and price.

   b) The system adds the price of the item to the total.

 end loop

7. The customer service representative gets payment information from the customer and enters it into the system.

8. The customer service representative submits the order to the system.

9. The system saves the order as pending, and forwards payment information to the accounting system.

10. When payment is confirmed, the order is marked confirmed, an order ID is returned to the customer, and the use case ends.

Alternatively, Place Order can be written as a complete flow of events. In that case, Place Web Order and Place Telephone Order just describe how they differ from Place Order (see Exhibits 4-17 through 4-19).

INTERFACES

Interfaces can be defined for actors, use cases, or both. An interface tells what we expect the entity to do. The interface is not part of the actor or the use case; rather, it is a description of how to interact with the actor or use case. You can have more than one interface for any actor or use case.

Exhibit 4-16 Place Web Order Use Case

1. The use case begins when the customer selects Place Order on the National Widgets home page.

2. The system displays the online catalog main page.

3. The customer browses the online catalog and selects products to purchase.

4. For each product selected

    a) the system displays a product description and price.

    b) the customer chooses to add the product to the shopping cart.

    c) the system adds the price of the item to the shopping cart total.

end loop

5. The customer chooses purchase.

6. The system prompts the customer to enter username and password.

7. The customer enters a username and password and selects Submit.

8. The system displays the shipping address and payment method for this customer's account.

9. The customer selects OK.

10. The system saves the order as pending, and forwards payment information to the e-commerce system.

11. When payment is confirmed, the order is marked confirmed, an order ID is returned to the customer, and the use case ends.

Exhibit 4-17 Place Order Use Case

1. The use case begins when the customer selects Place Order.

2. The customer enters his or her name and address.

3. The customer enters product codes for the products to be ordered.

4. For each product code entered

    a) The system supplies a product description and price.

    b) The system adds the price of the item to the total.

end loop

5. The customer enters credit card payment information.

6. The customer selects Submit.

7. The system verifies the information, saves the order as pending, and forwards payment information to the accounting system.

8. When payment is confirmed, the order is marked confirmed, an order ID is returned to the customer, and the use case ends.

Exhibit 4-18 Place Telephone Order Use Case

This use case is the same as Place Order except:

The customer gives all information to the customers service representative, who enters it into the system.

In step 2, the customer supplies a catalog ID that is used to get customer account information from the database. The customer service representative verifies the information with the customer.

In step 7, shipping information does not need to be verified.

Exhibit 4-19 Place Web Order Use Case

This use case is the same as Place Order except:

Step 2 is removed.

In step 3, the customer selects products by browsing an online catalog instead of entering product codes.

In step 4a, the system displays the information, and the customer chooses to add the item to a shopping cart.

In step 4b, the total is associated with a shopping cart.

In step 5 and 6, the customer logs into the system, and the system supplies the shipping address and payment information for that customer's account.

In step 7, shipping information does not need to be verified. The payment is sent to an e-commerce package.

The first step is to define the interface. An interface has a name and a set of operation signatures. An operation signature tells us what kind of data is passed with the operation and what kind of data is returned when the operation is complete. The operation tells what we expect the entity to do.

Consider first interface on Actors. Looking at Place Order, we find a need to get product descriptions and prices. These will come from the Inventory System actor. We define an interface for the Inventory System (see Exhibit 4-20).

The Inventory System actor interacts with a number of use cases. We could put all the behavior in the Product Info interface. Or we could define separate interfaces for the different kinds of behavior we expect from the Inventory System. If we look at Return Product, we see there is additional behavior for the Inventory System—adding products back to inventory. We could add the new behavior the the Product Info interface (see Exhibit 4-21), or we could define a new interface for this behavior (see Exhibit 4-22).

Exhibit 4-20 Interface Example for the Inventory System Actor

Product Info Interface

Get Product Description and Price (Product ID) return Description, Price, Quantity on Hand

Get Product ID and Price (Description) return Product ID, Price, Quantity on Hand

Exhibit 4-21 One Large Interface for Inventory System Actor

Inventory System Interface

Get Product Description and Price (Product ID) return Description, Price, Quantity on Hand

Get Product ID and Price (Description) return Product ID, Price, Quantity on Hand

Increment Stock (Product ID, Quantity)

Decrement Stock (Product ID, Quantity)

Exhibit 4-22 Adding a New Interface for Additional Behavior

Update Stock Interface

Increment Stock (Product ID, Quantity)

Decrement Stock (Product ID, Quantity)

We favor using a larger number of small interfaces. This makes the system more flexible to change in future. An entire interface can be added or removed easily, rather than changing an existing interface. You also may want to use the same interface with more than one actor or use case. Keeping the interface small makes it more reusable. So we would add the extra interface for the Inventory System actor rather than putting it in with the Product Info interface.

Now that we have defined the interfaces, we want to add them to the use case diagram (Exhibit 4-23). The straight line between the actor and the interface means the actor supports the interface. The dashed arrow indicates the use case which uses the interface.

If our actor is not a person, the interface will be the exact programmatic commands we use to interface with that actor. For example, if the actor is a network, the interface might be TCP/IP commands. If the actor is the inventory system that our order-processing software interfaces with, we need to find out what commands can be sent to the inventory system software. Those

Exhibit 4-23   Example of Interfaces

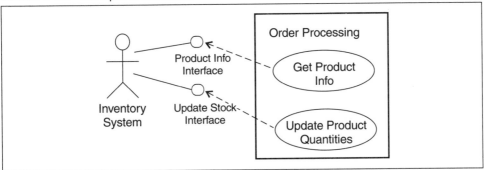

commands will define the interface to the inventory system actor. For our purposes, we probably will only use a subset of all the possible commands that the inventory system can receive. So our interface will define only the subset that we need.

Now consider interfaces on use cases. Everything works the same as interfaces on Actors, except now we are defining a programmatic interface to our system that actors may use. For example, assume National Widgets has been approached to allow big companies to place orders through a batch process. The Place Order use case has to provide an interface that the big companies can call to place an order (see Exhibit 4-24). As on the interfaces for actors, any use case could support one or more interfaces.

Now that we have defined the interfaces, we want to add them to the use case diagram (see Exhibit 4-25). The straight line between the use case and the interface means the use case supports the interface. The dashed arrow indicates the actor which uses the interface.

Actors and use cases with interfaces have to support the behavior of the interface. We don't care how the behavior is implemented, as long as it conforms to the interface we have defined. So, for example, the Inventory System has to update product quantities. I don't care if that system updates data in a database, or if it just prints a message to the warehouse manager to update a total on a white board. As long as product quantities are correctly maintained, my order-processing system doesn't care how that is accomplished.

Exhibit 4-24   Interface Example for Place Order Use Case

Place Order Interface
Place Order For Products (Company ID, List of Products, Contact Person)

Exhibit 4-25 Example of Interfaces

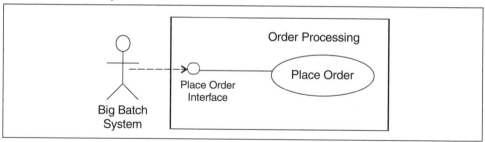

Because Place Web Order inherits from Place Order, it has to support the Place Order Interface. But it could implement the interface in a different way. The Place Order use case might implement the interface with SQL statements directly to a database, while Place Web Order might require the use of the e-commerce software when implementing the Place Order Interface.

You can use this mechanism of interfaces to support different levels of access to the system. Thus, when the customer places an order, the implementation of the interfaces might restrict his or her access to the system. When the customer rep places an order, the implementation of the same interfaces will be different and will allow access to more of the system.

Let's take the use case diagram for National Widgets from Chapter 3 and apply these techniques to make the diagram easier to read.

"Hey, Gus," Lisa said. "You promised to show us how to make our use case diagram less messy. Can we do it now?"

"Yes, it's really starting to bug me," Tara chimed in.

"Okay," Gus replied. "We'll add in inheritance between our Customer and Customer Rep actors to get rid of a bunch of the lines."

"Well, that's a good starting point," Dennis said after the changes had been made. "But from our use case documents, it looks like Update Product Quantities really is part of a lot of our use cases. Shouldn't that be broken out and made into an include relationship?"

"You're right. And there are some other include relationships too," Gus said. "Let's look over all our descriptions and update the diagram to match." [See Exhibit 4-26.]

Exhibit 4-26 Order-Processing Use Cases

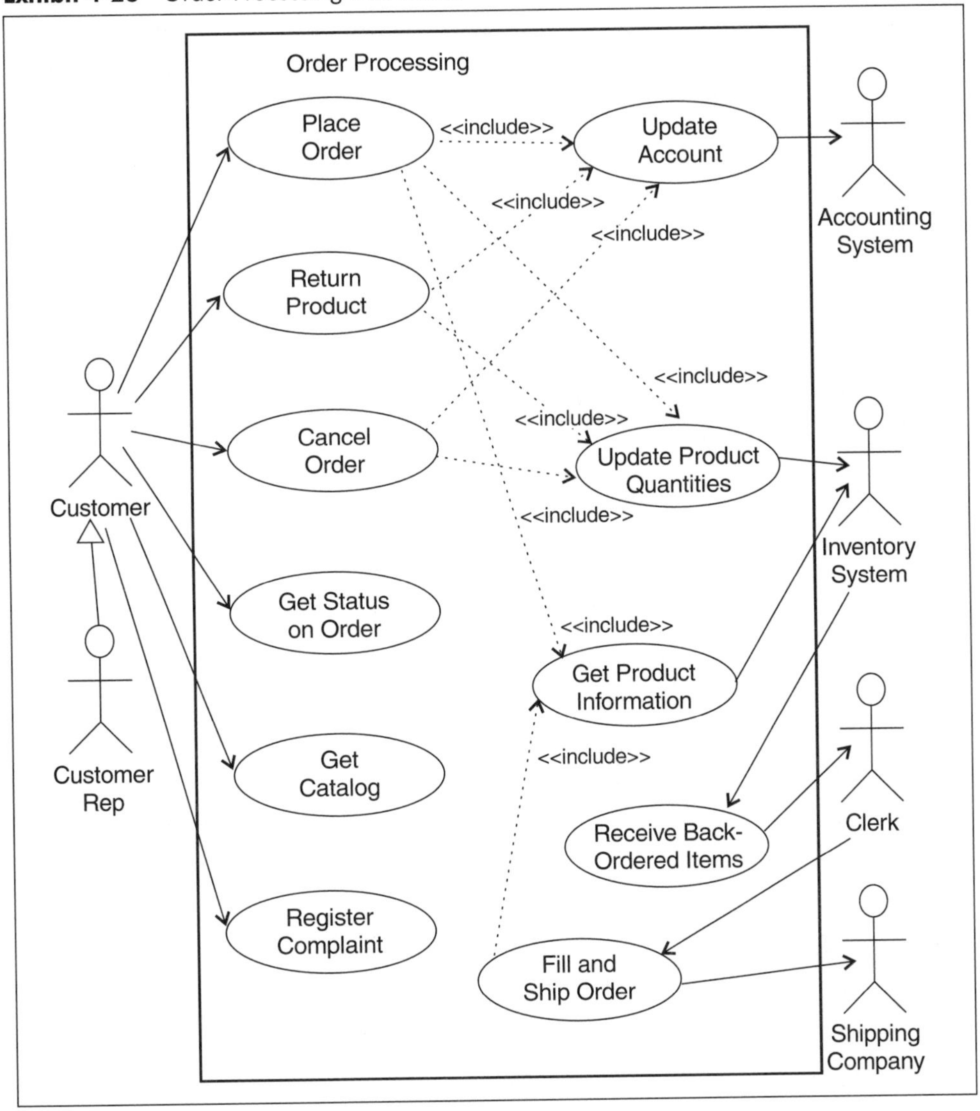

CHAPTER REVIEW

Use extend, include, inheritance, and interfaces to add clarity to your documentation and diagrams. After applying these techniques, the goal is to end up with easier-to-read documentation that more closely matches how things are really done, or how you want them to be done. You won't use all of these techniques all the time. And you won't use them when you first start defining use cases. Like our example problem, you will get the basic use case and relationships defined first, then you will apply some of these techniques to add information or make the documentation easier to understand.

Elaboration phase deliverables completed so far are shown in Table 4-1. Sometimes a written description of a use case or scenario can be hard to understand. This is especially true when you have a lot of branching or exceptions. In the next chapter we'll look at a simple way to diagram the steps of a use case. Diagrams can be used in place of text or to supplement the text descriptions.

Table 4-1 Elaboration Phase Deliverables

Complete	Deliverables
✔	Detailed basic path
✔	Alternative paths
	Activity diagrams
	User interface diagrammed (optional)
	Architecture
	Project plan

Chapter 5

Diagramming Use Cases

We have spent a lot of time writing text for our use cases. But as the old saying goes, a picture is worth a thousand words. In this chapter we'll look at three kinds of "pictures" we can use to add detail to, or clarify, our use cases. We'll use activity diagrams to document the steps of the use case. We'll add another section to the use case document for activity diagrams. We'll use simple sequence diagrams to show the actor-to-system interactions. These can also be added to the use case document. We'll use storyboarding to show the sequence of events from the user interface point of view. Storyboards take a lot of room, so we will put these in documents separate from the use cases, but referred to by the use cases. These pictures we create can be used with the text descriptions or in place of the text descriptions. Let clarity and good communication guide your choice of techniques.

ACTIVITY DIAGRAMS

 Activity diagrams have been used in many forms under many different names over the last few decades. The UML defines an activity diagram as a subset of a state diagram where most of the states are action states and most of the transitions are automatic. This sounds complicated, but the diagrams are actually very easy to use and read. They can be safely shared with customers, even those unfamiliar with software engineering. We'll start by looking at a simple activity diagram, then see how to extend it to show branching, repetition, and conditions.

"Hey, Gus," Lisa said. "I'm getting really tired of all this writing. Isn't there some easier way to show what these use cases do?"

"Sure. We can use activity diagrams to show the flow of events of the use case."

"What are activity diagrams, and if they are easier than use cases, why didn't we start with them?"

"Well," Gus said, "I felt we would get farther at the start if we wrote it in English, and there are some abilities, such as include and extend, that can't be shown in an activity diagram. Let's take our Place Order use case as an example." [See Exhibit 5-1.]

Gus continued, "Each activity in the use case will be represented by a rounded rectangle on a diagram. Transitions from one activity to another are represented by arrows." [See Exhibit 5-2.]

"Well, that looks okay, but it seems like some things are missing," Tara mused.

"Yeah," Dennis chimed in. "Don't we want to let customers order more than one product? And how can we show that we want to mark the order confirmed only if accounting approves?"

"We need to add conditions to our diagram, Gus," said Lisa, busily indicating places for conditions. [See Exhibit 5-3.] "They go in square brackets, so let's add them where we need them. I think I'll replace the action Select Place Order with a condition, so we don't have to go directly to placing an order every time we log in."

Exhibit 5-1 Place Order Use Case

1. The use case begins when the customer selects Place Order.

2. The customer enters his or her name and address.

3. If the customer enters only the zip code, the system supplies the city and state.

4. The customer enters product codes for products to be ordered.

5. For each product code entered

   a) The system supplies a product description and price.

   b) The system adds the price of the item to the total.

end loop

6. The customer enters credit card payment information.

7. The customer selects Submit.

8. The system verifies the information, saves the order as pending, and forwards payment information to the accounting system.

9. When payment is confirmed, the order is marked confirmed, an order ID is returned to the customer, and the use case ends.

Exhibit 5-2 Simple Activity Diagram Example

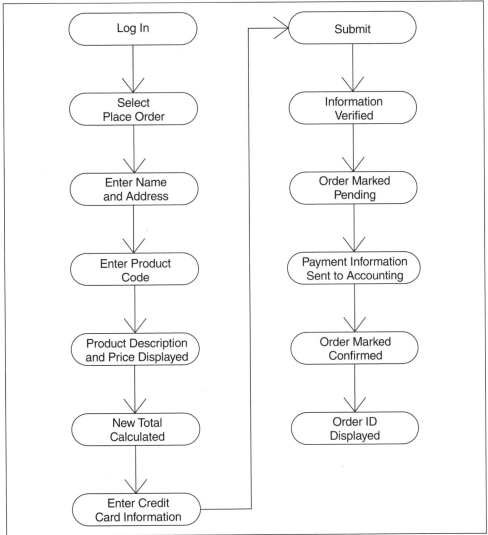

"Good idea, Lisa!"

"Okay, Lisa," Tara said. "Explain to me what all the new symbols mean."

"Well, the phrases in square brackets are conditions. That means we can take that path only if the condition is true. So after Log In, we can't get to Order Form Displayed until the user selects Place Order. The condition stops us from going down that path until it is true."

"That's what we want," Dennis laughed. "But what about the bullet and the bull's-eye?"

Exhibit 5-3 Activity Diagram—Conditional Example

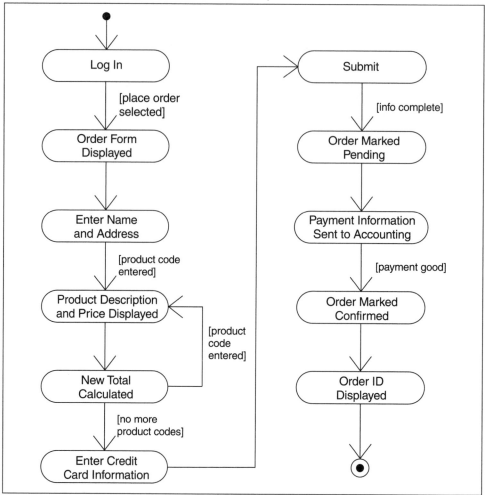

"The bullet is the starting point. The bull's-eye is the stopping point. On our diagram it was pretty clear where to start and stop, but if the diagram gets more complicated, we'll have to show them explicitly."

"That's looking more like it. Hey, Lisa! We have a bunch of different options from Log In. Do we show them all the same way?"

"We could, but I think it would be easier to show a decision point. That way the diagram will show clearly that we have to make a choice at this point. I'll redo part of the diagram so you can see it. We can use the decision point anywhere we have a decision to make. It's represented by a diamond." [See Exhibit 5-4.]

"Can we have only two arrows coming out of the diamond?"

Exhibit 5-4 Activity Diagram—Decision Point Example

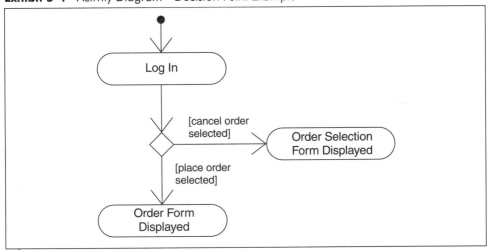

"No. You can have as many arrows as you want coming out of the diamond, but they all have to be labeled with conditions. You also can have as many arrows as you want coming into the diamond."

"I like these diagrams. I think it will be easier to show our alternatives for error handling or multiple decision points in this diagram rather than in text. Let's try some more use cases."

So far, everything we've shown allows for only one thread of activity. What if you want to allow multiple, parallel activities? Say, for example, that we allow a customer to bring up only one screen at a time. But when a customer rep logs in, we want all the different kinds of screens to come up at once, so when a customer calls, the rep doesn't have to wait while a screen is displayed. With the decision point we just discussed, we have to pick one choice. Exhibit 5-5 shows the diagram drawn with something called a fork.

The heavy line is the fork point. At this point the single path from Log In divides into two parallel paths. We are now allowing the order form and the order selection form to be displayed at the same time. Why is it called a fork instead of something like a separation or a divide? Think of a table fork with one handle that divides into multiple tines. The fork diagram in Exhibit 5-5 looks a little like a table fork. You can have as many paths coming out of the fork as you would like. There is only one path coming into the fork.

Similarly, we can show when multiple paths join back together. This is actually called a *join*. It looks like the fork, except we will have multiple paths coming into the join and one path coming out of the join. Let's assume that all the screens for the customer rep have to be closed before the rep can log off.

Exhibit 5-5 Activity Diagram—Fork Example

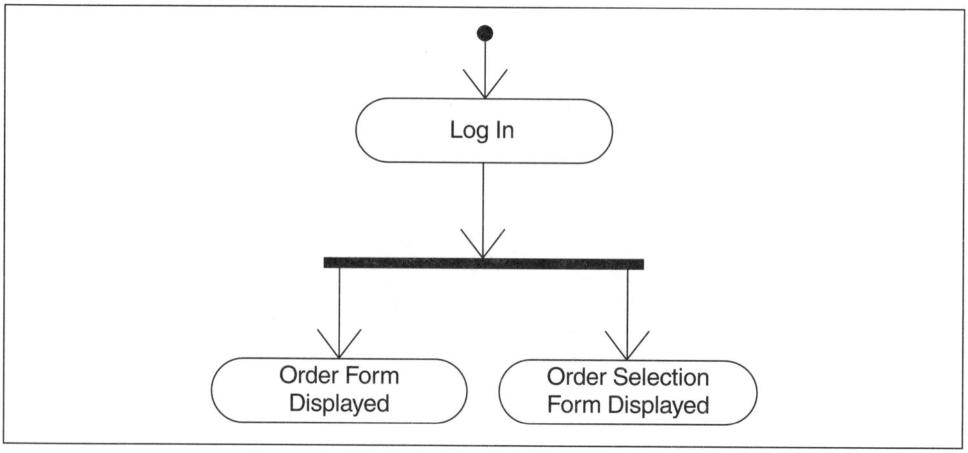

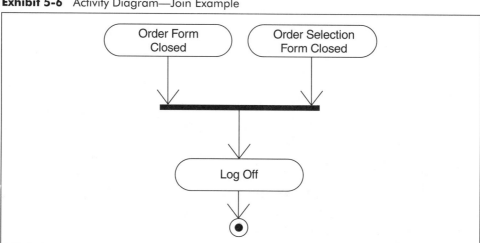

In Exhibit 5-6, we will not get to Log Off until both screens have closed. We wait at the join point until all the paths coming into the join have arrived, then we continue.

What we've shown in these activity diagrams is a subset of what is possible. This much will allow you to diagram the use cases. The things we can add to this diagram later include objects that handle the activities on the diagram, subsystems that handle the activities on the diagram, and message and signal passing. Because we aren't working with any of those things right now, we won't go into that notation.

Exhibit 5-6 Activity Diagram—Join Example

If you find that the diagram is getting really large and complex, split it into pieces. The rounded rectangle representing the activity actually could take the place of a whole diagram.

In Exhibit 5-7, Cancel Order Process can be another complete activity diagram showing the events for canceling an order. This way, we can see its relationship to logging in and that it is one of several options without having to put all the details in this diagram.

SIMPLE SEQUENCE DIAGRAMS

Some projects want a diagram that emphasizes the actor interactions with the system. You can use a simple sequence diagram for this purpose. Sequence diagrams show the entities that interact to do a job and the messages they share. Sequence diagrams are ordered by time. The bottom of the diagram is later in time than the top.

A simple sequence diagram includes all the actors across the top of the page and one object to represent the whole system. Below each entity is a dashed line representing the lifetime of the entity. The statements of the use case are put in the diagram as messages between the actors and the system. Exhibit 5-8 shows a simple sequence diagram for part of place order. Behavior in the use case is usually shown as a message between an actor and the system object. But any behavior performed internally by the system shows up as messages from the system to itself.

Notice how we handle a display to the customer. Message number 9.2, Display Order ID, is going from the system to itself. This is because you would

Exhibit 5-7 Activity Diagram—Referencing Other Diagrams Example

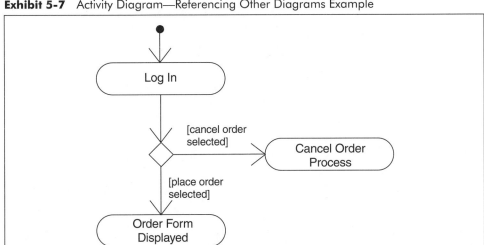

Exhibit 5-8 Simple Sequence Diagram for Place Order

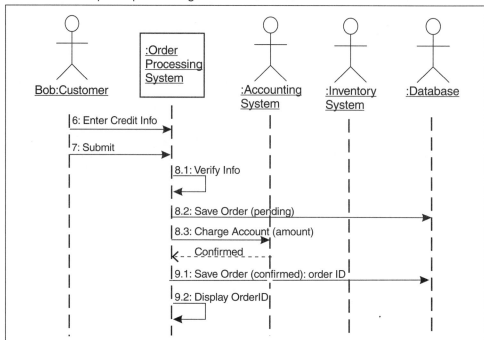

not ask a person to display something on a computer screen. Rather, the system displays something and the person views it. There is no human–system interaction at this point.

We have shown returned values in two ways. Message number 8.3, Charge Account, has a return value of confirmed. This is shown with a dashed line. There is no sequence number on the returned value, since this is not a message but a response to a message. Message number 9.1, Save Order, has a return value of order ID. In this case we showed the return value as part of the message.

In this example, the message sequence numbers are the same as the steps in the use case to emphasize the relationship. You may choose to do the same, or to number the messages in the diagram sequentially, without trying to maintain a relationship to the use case numbering.

Sequence diagrams can be much more complex. This simplified version is useful for situations where you want to emphasize the interactions between the actors and the system. We show more complex sequence diagrams in Chapter 9.

DIAGRAMMING THE USER INTERFACE

In some projects the user interface is critical to the project. For example, let's suppose National Widgets is going to do all its business through the Web. In such a case, you should diagram the user interface early in the process. This sample of the user interface can be shared with potential users early in the project in order to find any serious problems with it. You also may find new requirements, such as restricting who can log in to the system. It can also help your team clarify issues or problems found when trying to write or diagram the flow of events.

The user interface can be diagrammed as a storyboard. A storyboard is a series of drawings. The first drawing shows what the user interface looks like at the start. Each time there is a significant change to the look of the interface, a new drawing is made showing the updated interface.

"Hey, Gus."

"Yes, Dennis?"

"I'm not a real abstract thinker, so I'm getting confused trying to figure out what the user is doing in front of the screen. Do you have a nifty diagram someone like me can use to see what the user interface is like?"

"I do have an idea for you, Dennis. It comes out of the movie industry and is called storyboarding. What we'll do is draw pictures of the user interface at key points in the process."

"How do I know what the key points are?"

"Any time there is a significant change to the user interface, we'll do a new picture. Let's use our typical example of placing an order and storyboard it so you can see if you like the technique." [See Exhibits 5-9, 5-10, and 5-11.]

"Hey, wait," Tara exclaimed. "How does our customer know what to order? Does he have a catalog in his hands? What if he wants to look at it online? I think we need another selection on the first screen after login to look at the catalog."

"Can we make people enter a name and address first, before they can do anything else?" Dennis asked. "That way they can't forget to put in that information once they've ordered."

"Well, I think we should allow people to pick products right out of the catalog and have the order form filled in automatically."

"What about storing things like customer name, address, and credit card info, so frequent customers don't have to enter it all the time?"

"See how many ideas we've come up with just from looking at this one sequence?" Gus asked. "Now we need to look at those ideas to see if they are feasible and if we

Exhibit 5-9 Storyboard Example 1—First Screen Our User Will See

Welcome to National Widgets On-Line Catalog

**Please Enter Your Username and Password
to Access Our Electronic Catalog**

Username: _____

Password: _____

Exhibit 5-10 Storyboard Example 2—A Screen After Successful Login

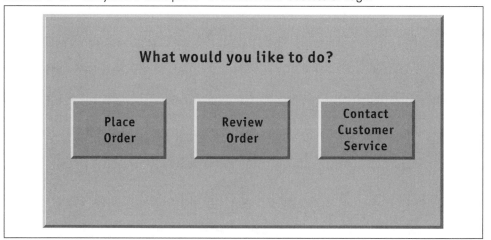

What would you like to do?

| Place Order | Review Order | Contact Customer Service |

want to include them in our first order-processing system. Maybe some of them will be later improvements. Even though they're all good ideas, we may not be able to do everything we would like in the first release of our product."

A storyboard will give your users a good idea of how the user interface works. This will allow your users to give you feedback on what they like or don't like. The storyboard is not designed to show the users a particular look and feel, but rather to show how well the events in a use case flow from a user perspective. It also will help you find alternatives that may not have been obvious from the written text.

Exhibit 5-11 Storyboard Example 3—A Screen After Selecting Place Order

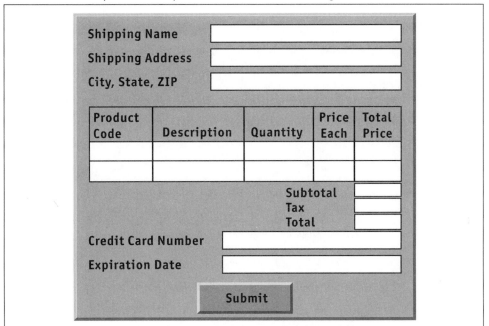

Using a software tool to design the user screens as they actually will appear is appealing because users can try out the interface directly on the computer. This can be a fairly quick process, but there is a danger that the users will not understand that there is no functionality behind the screens. The system isn't really placing orders; it just looks like it is because the screens are all complete. The danger is that your customers or users will think the system is already built. Set their expectations appropriately before letting them use actual screens.

CHAPTER REVIEW

Using activity diagrams to depict use cases sometimes can lead to more clarity than trying to describe the same thing in text. Or you may like using text for the use cases but decide to supplement the text with a few activity diagrams for key parts of the process. Simple sequence diagrams are used to focus on the actor-to-system interactions. They supplement the use case text.

You may also find it useful to storyboard the user interface to help clarify what is happening from the user's point of view. Or you may need to design the user interface early to get acceptance from customers or end users. Using a storyboard lets the user test the flow without being bound to a particular tool, or look-and-feel standard.

Using software tools to design the user interface is quick and allows end users to try the actual screens as they will appear in the application. The danger is that the user will think the system is complete when all you really have is a bunch of pretty screens. Table 5-1 shows what should be complete now.

In the next chapter we will consider the appropriate level of detail for a use case and how to manage one use case at different levels of detail.

Table 5-1   Elaboration Phase Deliverables

Complete	Deliverables
✔	Detailed basic path
✔	Alternative paths
✔	Activity diagrams
✔	User interface diagrammed (optional)
	Architecture
	Project plan

Chapter 6

Level of Detail

Now that you know how to write use cases, we will look at setting the level of detail for a use case. We also need to consider what to do when we need to maintain more than one use case document, each one at a different level of detail. We have to make sure that all the documents stay consistent. In this chapter we will look at use cases at various levels of detail, with examples of the different use cases. We will also discuss ways of maintaining consistency between the documents.

DETERMINING THE LEVEL OF DETAIL

One question everyone asks is "How do we know when we have the right level of detail in our use cases?" There are no hard and fast rules, but there are guidelines. When determining the appropriate level of detail, consider the following questions:

- Who needs to read this document and approve it?
- Who needs to use this document?
- What use are we going to make of this document?

The use cases we have shown so far are at a middle level of detail—they describe software from the point of view of the actor who uses the system. However, you might want use cases for other audiences. For example, you might want a use case to describe business processes. Or you might want a use case that describes software from the point of view of developing the software.

"Hey, Gus," Lisa said. "How detailed should these use cases be?"

"That depends."

"On what?"

"Well," Gus said, "what are we going to do with these use cases?"

"Hold on, Gus," Tara interrupted. "I thought you were telling us what to do!"

"Sure. But we all have different needs. I'll want more detail to write the code for the system. Dennis won't need that much detail for a business process perspective."

Dennis, who had been following the conversation, asked, "Do you mean the end-to-end process of getting the product to the customer? I've really been wanting something like that, something that ties all the other use cases together."

"Each use case we've written describes some software we're developing," Gus explained. "But the pieces of software are only part of the whole process of getting an order to a customer. I'll call the whole process Order Products and document it as a use case." [See Exhibit 6-1.]

Gus continued. "This is a business process use case. See how the focus is on the order in which the things are done and what department is responsible? I didn't worry about how each department did its job. And from the customer's point of view this is describing the whole use case from the time they order until the time the product arrives. I can diagram this with an activity diagram as well." [See Exhibit 6-2.]

Exhibit 6-1   Order Products Use Case

1. The use case begins when the customer places an order for products with the customer service department.

2. The customer service department sends the payment information for the order to the accounting department.

3. The accounting department updates National Widgets' accounts and deposits the payments in the bank.

4. The customer service department sends the order to the warehouse department.

5. The warehouse department collects the items for the order and sends them with the shipping address to the shipping department.

6. The shipping department packages up the items with the shipping address and gives the package to a shipping company for delivery to the customer, and the use case ends.

Exhibit 6-2 Order Products Activity Diagram

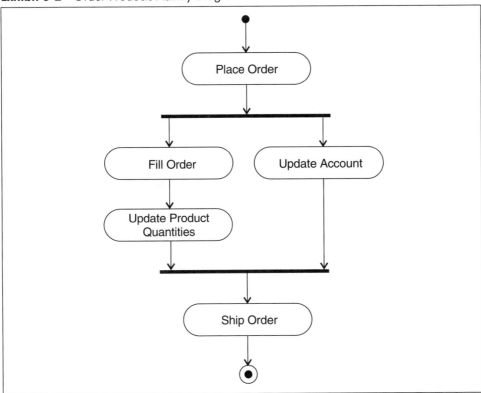

"That looks like an activity diagram, but why are our use cases on there?" Lisa asked.

"Any activity in an activity diagram can represent one small activity or a whole set of activities. For example, the Place Order activity represents a whole set of activities that are described by the Place Order use case. I didn't have to use the same name for the activity and the use case, but I like this way of naming the activities to make the relationship between them and the use cases explicit."

"Well, that looks okay, but could I describe the Place Order activity with another activity diagram?" Tara asked.

"Yes," Gus replied, "that's another way to represent the information. The Place Order activity can be represented by another activity diagram that shows how the Place Order activity is decomposed into lower-level activities. And the Place Order activity diagram is the activity diagram for the Place Order use case."

"Cool. I like how all the pieces relate to each other."

"Gus," Lisa called out, "I want to get back to the idea of detailed use cases for development."

"Good idea, Lisa! Let's go back and examine Place Order again." [See Exhibit 6-3.]

"Does this look complete from a customer point of view?"

"Yes," Lisa replied. "That seems to cover the basics of placing an order from my point of view as a customer."

"Okay. Now I'm going to play the role of developer," Gus said. "I need more information to develop the system. I have to write code for all the things the system is supposed to do. In step 3, where will the system get a city and state from when a zip code is supplied? Is this some table I have to create, does the information exist in a company database somewhere, do I have to buy software to supply that information, or am I expected to get the information from the U.S. Post Office? In step 5a, that looks like something the inventory system will supply but that should be explicitly stated. In step 8, what does 'verifies the information' mean? What is supposed to happen there? In step 9, what does 'payment is confirmed' mean? What is supposed to happen there? Also, when and how are the tax and shipping information calculated?"

"I had no idea there was so much information missing," Lisa exclaimed.

"Now, that depends on your point of view. The Order Products use case at the business process level answered Dennis's questions about how the parts of the company

Exhibit 6-3 Place Order Use Case—Actor View

1. The use case begins when the customer selects Place Order.

2. The customer enters his or her name and address.

3. If the customer enters only the zip code, the system supplies the city and state.

4. The customer enters product codes for products to be ordered.

5. For each product code entered

   a) the system supplies a product description and price.

   b) the system adds the price of the item to the total.

end loop

6. The customer enters credit card payment information.

7. The customer selects Submit.

8. The system verifies the information, saves the order as pending, and forwards payment information to the accounting system.

9. When payment is confirmed, the order is marked confirmed, an order ID is returned to the customer, and the use case ends.

work together and what order things have to happen. So, from the point of view of managing the process of ordering products, the Order Products use case is complete. Lisa, from your point of view as a customer, the Order Products use case is missing a lot of information about how you go about placing an order. But the Place Order use case, describing the actor view of the software, is the right level of detail for you. From my point of view as a developer, I like this version of Place Order, describing the developer view of the software." [See Exhibit 6-4.]

"There's a lot of information in here the customer doesn't care about. But we don't have to show this use case to a customer. This is for the developers to use to write code."

Exhibit 6-4   Place Order Use Case—Developer View

1. The use case begins when the customer selects Place Order.

2. The customer enters his or her name and address.

3. If the customer enters only the zip code, the system uses the zip code to query the U.S. Post Office online repository to get the city and state. The system adds the city and state to the order.

4. The customer enters product codes for products to be ordered.

5. For each product code entered

   a) The system uses the product code to query the inventory system software for a product description and price. The system adds the description and price to the order. The system queries the customer for product quantity. The customer enters a quantity for the product.

   b) The system adds the price of the item to the subtotal of the order.

end loop

6. The customer enters credit card payment information.

7. The customer selects Submit.

8. The system makes sure that all necessary data is entered, which must include a complete shipping address, credit card payment information, and at least one product. The system saves the order as pending and forwards payment information and the subtotal to the accounting system.

9. The accounting system calculates the tax and shipping amounts and returns a total for the order along with an indication of success in accepting the payment. The system marks the order confirmed, returns the total and an order ID to the customer, and the use case ends.

Different audiences have different needs when it comes to use cases, so you must know if are writing the use cases for managers, users, or developers. It really doesn't work to try to put all the different viewpoints together in one document. For one thing, it tends to make a very large document. It's easier to work with smaller documents. Another problem with putting everything together is that the use cases will be confusing to some of the people who have to read them and use them.

Once written, use cases have a variety of purposes. It is good to consider those purposes when determining the level of detail in the use case. Is the use case being written to describe the basic requirements of the system as part of a contract with a customer? Will it be used to create white box test plans or black box test plans or both? Will it be used to create user manuals for software? Will it be used to document new corporate processes? Or will it be used to develop software? If the answer is all of these, then you need more than one version of each use case.

TRACEABILITY BETWEEN USE CASES

Some companies have only one version of each use case. They just continually evolve the use cases, adding more detail over time, but do not save previous versions. Other companies maintain multiple versions of the same use case for different reasons. One version of the use case could be at a business-process level to help define corporate policies and procedures. Another version of the use case could be kept to create user manuals of the software and white box test plans. And yet another version of the use case could be given to development staff to create the software and black box test plans.

When different versions of the same use case need to be kept for different purposes, you may have a problem keeping them all up to date with each other. The larger your system is, the larger the problem of keeping all the documentation consistent.

"Hey, Gus."

"Yes, Dennis?"

"You had some stuff in the developer view of the use case that wasn't in the actor view. But I think something like indicating product quantity should go into the actor view of the use case, because it's something the customer has to do."

"You're right. The original use case didn't include a place to enter the product quantity ordered, but in writing the developer view of the use case, we found that capability was missing. It's something that the customer has to do, so we'll go back and add that new information to the actor view of the Place Order use case."

"Gus," Lisa queried. "Couldn't this get to be a maintenance problem? As we write the developer view of the use case, how do we make sure that the actor view gets updated, and maybe the business process use case as well?"

When you have multiple versions of the same use case, you have to be able to trace information from one version to another. That's why the Order Products use case includes the statement "The use case begins when the customer places an order for products with the customer service department." We should be able to trace that requirement at the business-process level to the Place Order use case. We should also be able to trace the Place Order use case to the first step in the Order Products use case.

What does that mean, to trace a requirement? It means that given one thing, you can find the other. So given the requirement in step 1 of Order Products, we can find the use case Place Order. Given the use case Place Order, we can find step 1 of Order Products. Establishing this relationship is what makes it possible to maintain consistency in the use cases.

There are various ways to create this relationship. Requirements management tools allow you to enter the various documents you have created into the tool and to create relationships between the use cases at various levels. You can do this with HTML by setting up hyperlinks between the use cases. For example, in Order Products step 1 you create a hyperlink to the Place Order use case document. Similarly, in the Place Order use case, you create a hyperlink back to the Order Products use case document, step 1.

Creating the relationships is tedious. But once the relationships exist in a tool or through hyperlinking documents, you have an easy way to find all the things that can be affected by a change to a particular document. If something being changed has a hyperlink to something else, you can follow the link to find out what else may have to change.

USE CASES FOR BUSINESS PROCESSES

Let's revisit using use cases to document business processes. In Exhibits 6-1 and 6-2, the business process was written as a use case and documented with an activity diagram. There is additional notation for the business-process use case in the use case diagram. The diagram for the Order Products use case (see Exhibit 6-2) thus looks like Exhibit 6-5. The relationships include, extend,

Exhibit 6-5 Order Products Use Case Diagram

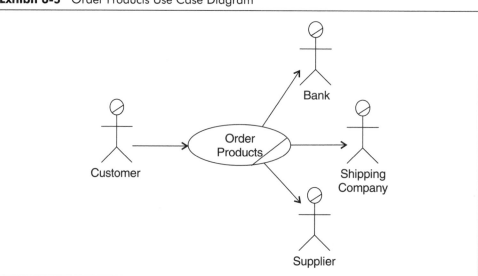

and generalization are all legal in business process use case diagrams, and work the same as in system use cases diagrams.

The actors look a little different. They are business actors, entities that exist outside our company. The Supplier actor in this diagram is contacted in an alternative to the use case when National Widgets is out of stock of an item, and therefore the item has to be ordered from a supplier so that we can send it to the customer.

The use case also looks a little different. This is a business process use case, describing the processes our company uses to satisfy the requests of the business actors. Remember that a use case is a complete sequence of steps that provides a result of value to an actor. The Customer business actor requests products; the Order Products Business use case is complete when that Customer receives his products.

A business process use case can include manual processes and physical entities such as paper forms and software. It can also indicate the people inside the company who perform the business processes. You can use a team collaboration diagram to show the entities that interact to execute the business process use case. One entity is the business worker, who is a person inside the company. The other kind of entity is the business entity. This is something used by the business worker to do his or her job. The business workers look similar to actors, the business entities are the circles with a line below them (see Exhibit 6-6). Finally, you can show the organizational units and how they interact (see Exhibit 6-7).

Exhibit 6-6 Order Products Team Collaboration Diagram

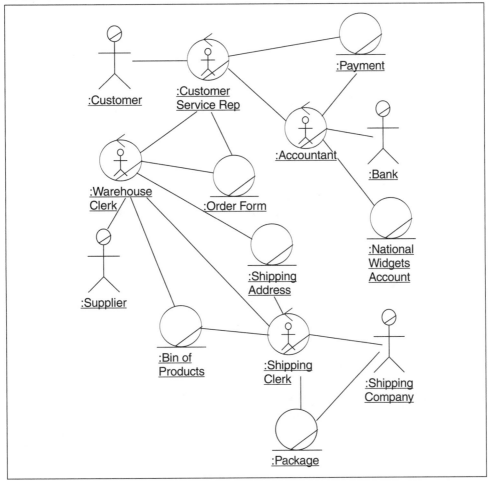

CHAPTER REVIEW

Deciding how much detail to put in a use case is an important factor for all projects. Determine who needs the use case and how it will be used. That information will help you set the use case level of detail.

You may want use cases for company managers, for end users, or for developers. The use cases may be used to create various documents at different levels of detail, such as corporate procedures, user manuals for software, white box test plans, or black box test plans.

Decide if you need to maintain multiple versions of the same use case at different levels of detail. If you do, then you need to determine a way to create

Exhibit 6-7 National Widgets Organizational Units

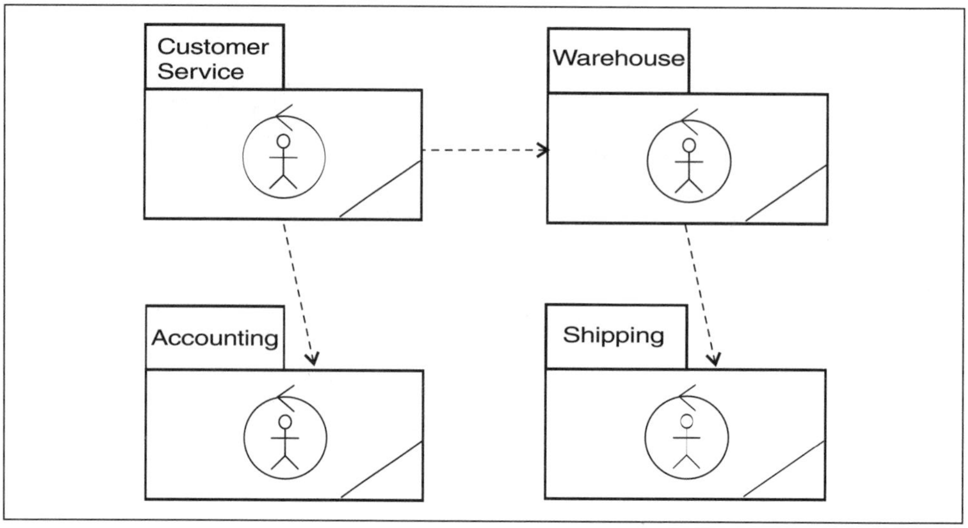

relationships between the various versions of the use case to make maintainence easier.

Requirements management tools may be used to create relationships between versions of use cases. You can use HTML documents and hyperlinks as an inexpensive way to achieve the same results.

Creating the relationships between use cases is tedious, but it makes maintenance easier, therefore making it more likely that the use cases will stay consistent as changes are made.

Table 6-1 indicates the elaboration phase deliverables that should be complete at this point. The next chapter considers the various documents that should be created for a project.

Table 6-1 Elaboration Phase Deliverables

Complete	Deliverables
✔	Detailed basic path
✔	Alternative paths
✔	Activity diagrams
✔	User interface diagrammed (optional)
	Architecture
	Project plan

Chapter 7

Documenting Use Cases

A lot of documentation is associated with use cases and needs to be organized somehow. You want the documentation to be understandable but you want other things as well. For example, you may want to be able to trace from system-level to subordinate use cases or from use cases to scenarios to test plans. You may want to be able to set priority levels on a use case or on any part of it and later run a report listing all use cases of a certain priority. Or you may want to be able to set and check status on a use case, such as whether it has been coded or tested.

In this chapter, we'll look at a sample use case template and consider different methods for implementing it. Every author has a favorite template. Our suggestion is to look over several, choose the format that works best for your company, and use it consistently.

DOCUMENTATION TEMPLATES

Any project will include a variety of documents for sharing information. These may be simple or complex, depending on the needs of the project. What follows are some sample documentation templates. We start with an overall system description (see Exhibit 7-1). You will have just one of these documents. It probably will be in a file or document by itself.

Next, we need descriptions for the use cases. Each use case most likely will be in a document or file by itself. If a use case has a lot of detailed alternative descriptions, they also might be in separate files. First is a very detailed use case document template, as seen in Exhibit 7-2(a) and 7-2(b). You will have one for each system-level use case. You also will have one for each subordinate

Exhibit 7-1 System Description Document Template

System Name

<A brief description. In a large system, this can be several pages. Note that this is not meant to be detailed requirements, but rather a basic overview of the system.>

Risk Factors

<List risk factors for the project in priority order.>

System-Level Use Case Diagram

<One or more use case diagrams showing all the use cases and actors in the system. This does not have to include relationships between use cases such as include, extend, or generalization.>

Architecture Diagram

<Include a description of the interfaces as well. These could be on the diagram or listed in text.>

Subsystem Descriptions

<Include a brief description of each subsystem.>

Exhibit 7-2(a) Detailed Use Case Description Document Template

---

Use Case Name

Brief Description

<Usually a paragraph or less. May include the priority and status of this use case.>

Context Diagram

<A small use case diagram showing this use case and all of its relationships.>

Preconditions

<A list of conditions that must be true before the use case starts.>

Flow of Events

<A section for the basic path and each alternative path.>

Postconditions

<A list of conditions that must be true when the use case ends, no matter which path is executed.>

Subordinate Use Cases Diagram

<A small use case diagram showing the subordinate use cases of this use case.>

Subordinate Use Cases

<A section for each subordinate use case with its flow of events.>

Exhibit 7-2(b) Detailed Use Case Description Document Template

Activity Diagram
<An activity diagram of the flow of events or some significant or complex part of the flow of events.>

View of Participating Classes
<A class diagram showing the classes that collaborate to implement this use case.>

Sequence Diagrams
<One or more sequence diagrams for the basic path and alternatives.>

User Interface
<Sketches or screen shots showing the user interface—possibly storyboards.>

Business Rules
<A list of the business rules implemented by this use case.>

Special Requirements
<A list of the special requirements that pertain to this one use case—for example, timing, sizing, or usability.>

Other Artifacts
<These can include references to the subsystem the use case belongs to, an analysis model, a design model, code, or test plans.>

Outstanding Issues
<A list of questions pertaining to this use case that need to be answered.>

use case. You will need a similar document for the detailed alternatives. Just leave out the parts that are unnecessary or redundant. These templates also are shown in Appendix B. A complete set of documents for the Order Processing System is in Appendix E.

You don't have to include all these sections. If your use cases are not this complex, then you don't need all these sections. You may find you want additional sections. That's fine. This is just a sample given as a starting point. If it works as is, use it; otherwise, modify as needed.

OTHER DOCUMENTS

We frequently move some of the sections of the use case document into other documents. For example, you may want all the user interface screen shots together in a document separate from the use cases. Or you may want to collect all the special requirements together in one document, rather than scattering them throughout the use case documents. It's good to have a template for these other documents as well, so everyone knows what kind of information to include in the document. The documents we create to go along with the use case documents are non-functional requirements, glossary, data definition, and user interface design.

Special requirements are frequently called non-functional requirements to distinguish them from the use cases that are the functional requirements. It is particularly important to have a template for the special requirements document so that the team understands what is meant by non-functional requirements. The template will also help you find all the non-functional requirements in your system. See Exhibit 7-3 for an example.

Exhibit 7-3   Non-functional Requirements Document Template

Usability

<What is known about the users of this system? Are they not used to computers, power users, or somewhere in between? How easy must this system be to use?>

System

<What kind of system will this software run on? Do we have to port to multiple platforms? Must the software support multiple simultaneous users?>

Security

<What are the needs for secure login or secure transmission of data?>

Persistence

<Do we have any persistent data? Are there any requirements on the database to use?>

Integration with Other Systems

<Does this software have to integrate with other software or hardware?>

Error Detection/Handling/Reporting

<Are errors allowed? What is a reasonable error rate? What are our requirements for prevention, detection, handling, and reporting of errors?>

Redundancy

<Are there any needs for redundant data, subsystems, processes, or hardware?>

Performance

<Are there any restrictions on how slow or fast the system or any part of it will run?>

Size

<Are there any restrictions on the size of the system or any part of it?>

Internationalization

<Does the software have to support any character set worldwide or only some of them? What information must be translated?>

We always recommend a glossary of terms. Don't assume that everyone knows what every term means or even that everyone has defined the same terms the same way. Create a glossary that all team members can access. See Exhibit 7-4 for an example.

A data definition document is also very helpful. This is a place to record information about the format of the data. For example, assume that a name is defined to be 50 characters. If you put that information in the use cases, then when you change the name to be 75 characters, you will have to review every use case looking for every 50-character name so it can be changed. Instead, put the size of a name in the data definition document, where anyone reading the use case who wants to know the size of a name can look up the information. If the size of the name changes, you only have to change that information in one place. Exhibit 7-5 has sample data definitions.

Finally, you may want a document for the user interface. One kind of user interface document is guidelines and standards. This can include requirements such as that every screen must include an exit button or that the standard font for applications is 12-point Arial. It might also include screen shots and navigation information.

Exhibit 7-4 Sample Glossary of Terms

Accounting System
A software system that tracks customer accounts and processes accounts receivable and accounts payable.

Manager
Anyone who gets reports from the Order Processing system.

Security
The need to control who has access to our software and databases.

Exhibit 7-5 Sample Data Definitions

City
An alphabetic string of no more than 30 characters. Strings are allowed to include a period and an apostrophe.

Product Price
A currency type field with two decimal places.

Tax
A currency type field calculated to 4 decimal places, but rounded to 2 decimal places.

TOOL SUPPORT FOR DOCUMENTS

Unless you are writing use cases on paper with pen, pencil, crayon, or whatever, you will have to look for some kind of tool support for your use case documents. Consider your needs before buying tools. Documents can be written with desktop publishing tools such as FrameMaker, word processing tools such as Microsoft Word, spreadsheets such as Microsoft Excel, HTML pages, or other Web-based formats, requirements management tools such as RequisitePro, groupware such as Lotus Notes, or e-mail programs. Or they may be stored in a relational database. Almost any tool can be used to generate and store use case documents, so you have to consider the needs of your team, project, and company.

Answer these questions before going tool shopping:

- Are you only looking for a way to record text?
- Do you need search capabilities?
- Do you need to share the documents with a small, large, or geographically distributed team?
- What about report generation? What kinds of reports do you want concerning your use cases?
- Do you want to be able to hyperlink from one part of a document to another part or to another document?
- Do the documents have to be shareable across multiple platforms?
- Do you need the ability to compose documents into books to get the right page numbering or chapter numbering across documents?
- What other tools need to use what is in the documents? How do you integrate with those tools?

After answering these questions you will be prepared to evaluate the tools you already have, as well as tools you are considering buying. One last thing to think about is ease of use. Hard-to-use tools tend to sit on a shelf unless there are no other options. In this case you have many options, so look for something your team will use.

We like using the Web for maintaining project documents. If possible, create a place on your corporate intranet for document storage and put all the documents in that area in HTML, with hyperlinks connecting related information. For example, project terms in the various documents can be linked to their definitions in the glossary. The top-level use case descriptions in the system document can be linked to their associated use case documents. Or data items can be linked to their descriptions in the data definition document. This makes it very easy to read and review project documents. And if the documents are electronic, you only have to update them on-line for everyone to get the changes automatically.

DOCUMENTING LOGIN

Many applications have a need to control access to the system. The question of how to handle login always comes up. In this section we describe four ways of documenting login in use cases: (1) login including the other use cases, (2) other use cases including login, (3) other use cases extending login, and (4) login independent of and a precondition for the other use cases.

The first method is to have a Log In use case that includes all of the other use cases that are secure. Exhibit 7-6 shows a use case diagram for this method using part of the order processing example. In addition to updating the diagram, we also have to write the text of the Log In use case (see Exhibit 7-7). None of the other use cases change.

This method is good because the use case diagram looks like what you would expect: The customer logs in, and from there he or she can access any of the allowed system functions. However, look at the text of the Log In use

Exhibit 7-6   Login Includes Other Use Cases

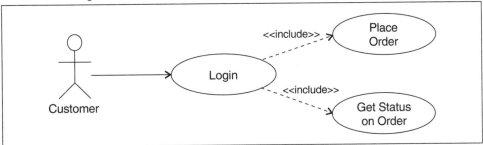

Exhibit 7-7   Log In Use Case

1. The use case begins when the customer starts the application.

2. The system prompts the customer to enter a username and password.

3. The customer enters a username and password.

4. The system verifies that this is a valid user.

5. While the customer does not select exit, do the following steps in any order.

6. The customer may choose to place an order (include Place Order).

7. The customer may choose to get the status on an order (include Get Status on Order).

end loop.

8. The use case ends.

case. If you want to add new use cases to the system, you will also have to change this use case. That is not good from a maintainence point of view, because it is easy to forget to make the change to login. Also, we don't like that fact that login now has to have knowledge of all the other parts of the system. We like the use cases to be as independent of each other as possible.

The next method is to have the other use cases include login. Again we update the use case diagram (see Exhibit 7-8) and the text (see Exhibits 7-9 and 7-10).

This method is good because the Log In use case describes login and nothing else. On the other hand, the Place Order use case and the use case diagram make it appear that the customer has to log in every time he or she wants to do something different. This will probably become very annoying to users over time.

The next method is to have the other use cases extend the login use case. Again we update the use case diagram (see Exhibit 7-11) and the text (see Exhibits 7-12 and 7-13).

Exhibit 7-8 Other Use Cases Include Login

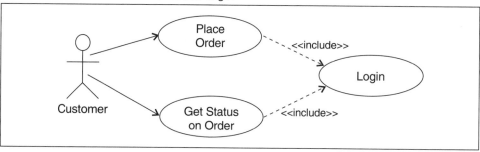

Exhibit 7-9 Log In Use Case

1. The use case begins when the customer starts the application.

2. The system prompts the customer to enter a username and password.

3. The customer enters a username and password.

4. The system verifies that this is a valid user.

5. The use case ends.

Exhibit 7-10 Partial Place Order Use Case

1. The use case begins when the customer logs in to the system (include Login).

2. ...

Exhibit 7-11 Other Use Cases Extend Login

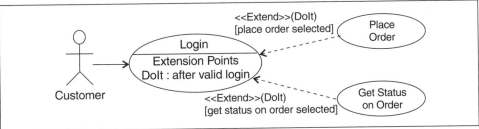

Exhibit 7-12 Log In Use Case

1. The use case begins when the customer starts the application.

2. The system prompts the customer to enter a username and password.

3. The customer enters a username and password.

4. The system verifies that this is a valid user.

5. While the customer does not select exit

6. Extension point: Do It.

end loop.

7. The use case ends.

Exhibit 7-13 Partial Place Order Use Case

Precondition: The customer has selected Place Order.

In Exhibit 7-11 we see that the customer logs in one time and from there gets access to the rest of the system. Log in adds an extension point, but that is all, you do not have to change it when adding new use cases.

So far, this looks like a good approach. The only drawback here is describing extend to the people who are reviewing this document. It can be a difficult relationship to explain, especially to people who are not developers.

Finally, the Log In use case can be completely independent of the other use cases, but we include a precondition in the other use cases that a valid user be logged in before they can be executed. Again, we update the use case diagram (see Exhibit 7-14) and the text (see Exhibits 7-15 and 7-16).

This method is good because Log In only describes login and nothing else. The diagram and the text are clear and easy to understand and we have the added benefit of more flexibility in the system. Now Place Order does not require login to execute, but just a valid user. Executing login is one way to get a valid user, but there may be other validation methods as well.

Exhibit 7-14 Log In as an Independent Use Case

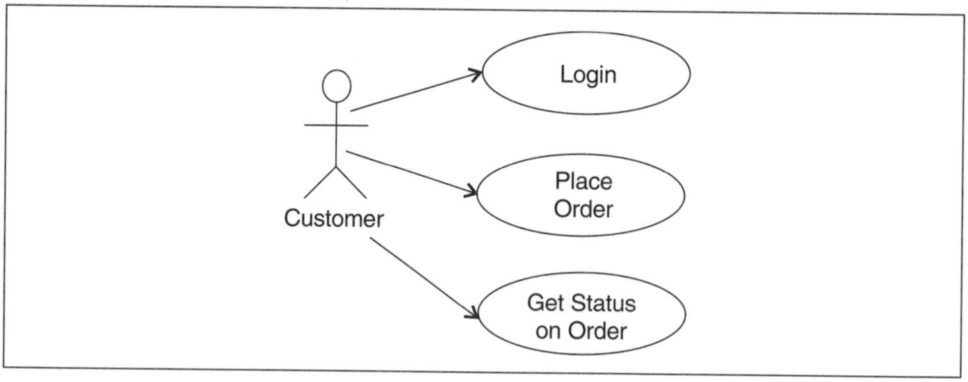

Exhibit 7-15 Log In Use Case

1. The use case begins when the customer starts the application.

2. The system prompts the customer to enter a username and password.

3. The customer enters a username and password.

4. The system verifies that this is a valid user.

5. The use case ends.

Exhibit 7-16 Partial Place Order Use Case

Precondition: A valid user has logged into the system.

Our favorite approach is the last one. It seems to be the easiest to read, and it has the most flexibility. However, all of the approaches are correct, so pick the one that works best for your projects.

DOCUMENTING CRUD

We always get questions on how to document create, read, update, and delete functionality known as CRUD. You will often need this kind of use case when your application includes maintaining data.

There are two basic approaches. One is to create a separate use case for each kind of access to the data. The other is to create one use case for a data type that embeds all of the CRUD functions.

Our order processing system uses the first approach. Thus, Place Order creates orders, Get Status on Order reads orders, Return Product updates orders, and Cancel Order deletes orders. Notice that we named the use case by the behavior that the user expects. We did not call the use cases Create

Order, Read Order, Update Order, and Delete Order. Instead, we used names that make sense to the users of the system. Also notice that all of these use cases have common functionality, captured using include relationships.

We could have made one use case called something like Maintain Orders, which would have been in charge of anything having to do with orders. However, this doesn't really make sense for this system. Different actors use separate CRUD functions, so it makes more sense to make them separate use cases. On the other hand, in some applications combining them may be sensible — for example, if the application is for a database administrator to update tables in a database. In the inventory system, you might want a use case called Maintain Inventory.

Our preference is to start with separate use cases for each of the CRUD functions and to name them in some way meaningful to the application. If some use cases are almost the same, we may choose to merge them to make them easier to read and maintain.

CHAPTER REVIEW

We did not develop any new material for our order-processing system in this chapter, but we did organize our material to make it easier to read, review, and maintain. You are not required to have documented your complete system at this point; however, you need enough information to develop a project plan and start on the first iteration of construction. Table 7-1 lists the elaboration phase deliverables that should now be complete. The next chapter discusses various ways to review use cases and include examples of common mistakes.

Table 7-1 Elaboration Phase Deliverables

Complete	Deliverables
✔	Detailed basic path
✔	Alternative paths
✔	Activity diagrams
✔	User interface diagrammed (optional)
	Architecture
	Project plan

Chapter 8

Reviews

Throughout the process of developing use cases, you will want periodic reviews of your work. These will help you find problems early. The earlier you find problems, the cheaper they are to fix, so a periodic review is worth the time it takes.

If you are already using a formal review process, continue doing so. The material in this section is not intended to be, or to replace, a formal review. It is included to stimulate thought about the review process.

Many different people with many different points of view might be interested in reviewing your use cases. They may include whoever is defining your requirements, such as a customer, a marketing department, or an advisory board. End users also will be interested in the use cases when they are the actors. They also probably will want to look at your user interface description. The architect and senior technical people will want to review the use cases, architecture, risk factors, and project plan. They will be looking for completeness, clarity, and feasibility. We'll look at the various kinds of review in this chapter.

REVIEW FOR COMPLETENESS

You will want a small team, including the project architect and one or more analysts, to go through the documentation to make sure it is complete and consistent.

Gus looked up from his pile of notes. "Hey, gang, let's take a break."

"Sounds good to me!"

"Great!"

"Thought we were going to work all night!"

"Wait a minute," Gus said. "Not quite what I meant. What I meant was, let's take a break from design and do a review."

"A review? But we've been working on it steadily! Why would we need a review?"

"Well, we have been working on it steadily and for quite a while now. What we need to do is go back and look it over again—to make sure everything still makes sense and that it's consistent. We've all been concentrating on making it work. Now we need to look at it from another viewpoint and see if it makes sense. Lisa, you're a developer now. Look over what we've documented and see if it's what you need to develop the software. Dennis! You're a user . . ."

"Oh, great. Let's see, that probably means that I want to look over everything as if I know nothing about how it works, just what I can 'see' when I use it."

"That's right! Tara, you and I will look for inconsistencies. Since this is fair-sized now, it may have been infected with 'Feeping Creaturism,' and we'll want to make sure it all makes sense."

"Feeping what?" Tara burst out.

"Feeping Creaturism. That's when features creep into a project and start running away with it. Any project that goes on in time has a tendency to gather new features. We'll go back and make sure they are actually needed and place a priority level on the ones that are."

Look at the project description, the risk factors, and the assumption list, and ask yourself the following questions:

- Does the project description still make sense?
- What other influencing factors have you discovered?
- Are the risks the same as you first thought? Did any go away? Are there new ones? Have the priorities changed?
- Have any assumptions become certainties? Are there any new assumptions?

Review your use case diagram and use case descriptions with the following questions in mind:

- Have you found any new actors? Are some of the actors not needed?

- Have any actors moved inside the system? Has anything inside the system moved out?
- Do the names and descriptions of the actors still make sense?
- Have you found any new use cases? Have you lost any?
- Do the names and descriptions of the use cases still make sense?
- Do you have at least a basic path for each of your use cases?
- Do you have alternative paths for all your use cases?
- Does the user interface diagram match the use cases?

All the documentation needs to be updated so that all parts are consistent with all the others.

REVIEW FOR POTENTIAL PROBLEMS

Now review the risk factors, market factors, and your exception alternatives. Again, you want to include the architect and one or more analysts. You are looking for the obvious problem areas in your system. For each problem discovered, determine where it can be resolved in your system. Look for groupings of problems across multiple use cases, things that affect the system as a whole.

For example, in the order-processing system, many of the exception scenarios refer to the inventory and accounting systems being unavailable. In this case we obviously need a mechanism to hold onto requests until the systems are back online. Find ways to handle these kinds of problems consistently across the system.

Resist the temptation to put in implementation details. For example, our customers need access to our system. Making that access a Web browser is an implementation detail. Instead, make a note that you need a way for customers to access the system and list the characteristics of that interface. Later you can decide the best way to handle it.

REVIEW WITH END USERS

You also will want to review the use cases and storyboards with people who will be using the system. The following are the primary questions:

- Does the system do what you expect?
- Is anything missing?
- Is there anything you don't need?
- Do you understand what the system does?

- Looking at the flows and the user interface, is the system comfortable to use?
- Does the system behave as you expect?

If user acceptance is a high risk for your project, it is important to do this review early to get acceptance from the users for your system.

REVIEW WITH CUSTOMERS

Review the list of assumptions and the use cases with whoever is defining the system, asking the following questions:

- Do you agree with the assumptions I've made?
- What needs to change?
- Do I really understand what you want?
- Is the system what you expect?
- Do you understand what the system does?

It's important to stabilize the requirements early in the process, before you have a lot invested in development. They will almost certainly change, but having stable requirements up front usually means that only minor changes will be necessary later.

REVIEW WITH DEVELOPMENT

Finally, review with the development team. Make sure everyone understands what the project is about. Keep these questions in mind:

- Does it all make sense?
- Can you build a system from the use case documents?
- What else do you need to know before you can start?

Get acceptance from your key technical people. Build their enthusiasm for this project.

REVIEWERS

Each of the review types just listed can be more or less formal. Some groups sit around a table with copies of the documents, pizza, and sodas, and review the documents together. Other groups spend several days giving formal presentations to customers, independent verification and validation groups, and management. Then they hold follow-up meetings to discuss problems discovered and their resolution. Or you may find something in between that is useful.

What makes a good reviewer? Some people are better at reviewing for technical content, others are better at reviewing for style, consistency, and clarity. You want both kinds of reviewers. The best reviewers are those who will be honest. A review period is for finding problems. Reviewers who are too nice are not helpful. On the other hand, you don't need brutal reviewers either! Remember, all the reviewers' comments are from their point of view. Not every comment will get incorporated into the documentation. You may want some reviewers from outside the project. Outsiders have an unbiased view and will be quick to spot areas that are unclear, inconsistent, or incomplete.

ADDING FLEXIBILITY TO YOUR SYSTEM

What if you have an overall goal that your system needs to be flexible enough to change? You might like to try the following exercise adapted from one by Stewart Brand, *How Buildings Learn.*

First, allocate one to two days for the exercise. It is best if this is offsite and the participants are undisturbed. Check your pagers and cell phones at the door, please! Then pick an exercise leader. Usually, the exercise leader is not part of the project. This person's job is to keep the exercise on track and focused on the issues. This is a good job for a skilled outside consultant.

The exercise leader spends a week or so before the exercise interviewing the major players in the project. This can include the project sponsor, senior management, the lead architect, or the senior technical staff. The exercise leader interviews these people to find out what they consider the major issues ("What keeps you awake at night?") and what their expectations are about the future of the system under development. The exercise leader also becomes familiar with the vocabulary of the project. What are the buzzwords and common expressions in use around the project?

Then the project sponsor, project manager, chief architect, and lead technical people gather for a one- to two-day session. Unless the project is huge, this should be five or fewer people plus the exercise leader. This is not an exercise for the whole project team. If your team has only five people, the project sponsor and the project manager join the exercise leader. If the project manager is not also the lead technical person, add that person to the group as well. The group needs the exercise leader's interview notes plus the project documentation that has been written to date.

The first day begins with identifying the need for the project ("Why are you building this system?"). This is not the same as the project description, which defines what you are building. This part of the exercise is exploring why you are building it.

Then the group explores the market forces that could affect this project. These include things such as changes in technology, regulation by various government agencies, what the competition is doing, customer demands, and changes in the customer base. The group ranks these market forces in terms of importance and uncertainty. The most important and most uncertain are at the top of the list. The important uncertainties could cause the failure of the project. The group also makes a list of what they consider to be reliable certainties for their project, such as new and faster systems coming out at least once a year.

Next, the group identifies and spells out the "official future" of the system, the one that everyone thinks they are supposed to expect ("We'll never have more than 5,000 users at a time."). The exercise leader has interview material as a starting point. Then the group takes the official future and modifies it using the list of important uncertainties. Each modification gives another possible future. The group ends up with a whole set of possible futures for the system.

In the next step, the group must start thinking the unthinkable. Let people top each other in imagining terrible and delightful things that might happen to your system ("Every baby boomer in the world signs up for an online account at once"). Use these to modify the official future. Add these new modifications to your set of possible futures. The goal is to find new, plausible futures that are surprising or even shocking.

Sleep on that. The next day the group revisits the futures, adjusts them, names them, and picks two to five of the most plausible. Using memorable names for the futures helps people recall them and differentiate between them. Of the two to five plausible futures, don't worry about which one is most likely to occur. Do include at least one wildcard future that is considered unlikely but horrifying. Write detailed, vivid stories for the futures to bring them to life.

Take the two to five plausible futures and storylines, and compare them to your project description, use case diagram, architecture diagram, and use case descriptions. What has to change to allow any of the two to five new futures to be handled, if they were to occur? Is it possible for the system to be made flexible enough to accommodate all the new possibilities? Look at the project scope and the project plan. Can these changes be incorporated in the time frame and budget allowed?

Go back to the project risk analysis. What new risks have you discovered? Do some regret analysis. Ask, "What if we get it wrong? What will we regret not having done? What will we regret locking in?"

Make decisions on what to keep in the project and what to change based on the exercise. Update all the documentation to reflect these decisions. Go back and share the results with the project team.

COMMON MISTAKES

We're going to leave National Widgets for a little while and look at some examples from other projects. These examples illustrate things that are commonly done wrong with use cases. We will discuss what is wrong with the use cases, and how to fix them.

Work Flow on a Use Case Diagram

A recording studio sells time in the studio to customers, as well as selling the tapes that are made and services such as editing or catering. This recording studio wanted to automate the existing manual processes for managing the studio time and work orders.

The first use case diagram they created looks like Exhibit 8-1. It seems to be reasonable, except for the arrows between the use cases. What are they supposed to represent? Talking with the development team, we discovered that the arrows represent work flow.

The Unified Modeling Language (UML) provides nine different diagrams, each with different information about the system being developed. Use case diagrams provide a static picture of the functionality of the system. Activity diagrams are used to show work flow.

What the recording studio needed was a combination of a use case diagram, to show functionality, and an activity diagram to show the work flow. We removed the arrows between the use cases in the use case diagram (see Exhibit 8-2). Then we created an activity diagram for the work flow. Notice that the activity diagram has activities with the same names as the use cases (see Exhibit 8-3). This activity diagram is at the level of business processes. It shows how the different pieces of software relate to each other. This activity diagram also includes an activity that is not software—the Give Work Order to Engineer.

When the use cases must execute in a certain order, when there are conditions that must be met between the execution of some use cases, or when you need to show manual processes mingled with the software, then use an activitiy diagram at the business process level. You can show this information in

Exhibit 8-1   Recording Studio Use Case Diagram

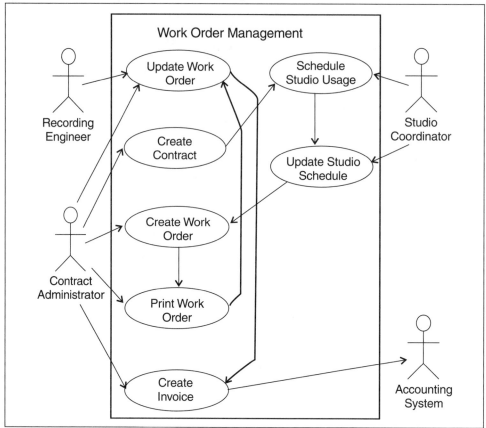

the use case text using mechanisms such as preconditions. But to find all the conditions you have to look at all the use cases. It is easier to show this information on an activity diagram. For completeness, include the preconditions in the use case document as well.

This work flow example illustrates that not all information can be, or should be, shown on a use case diagram. You will often need a combination of diagrams to get a complete picture of your system.

Use Cases Too Small

A company makes a switch that takes some number of video signals as input and outputs one video signal. It contains a variety of editing commands, such as cut from one signal to another, fade from one signal to another, add a background, or change the background color. This switch is used primarily in two

Exhibit 8-2 Corrected Recording Studio Use Case Diagram

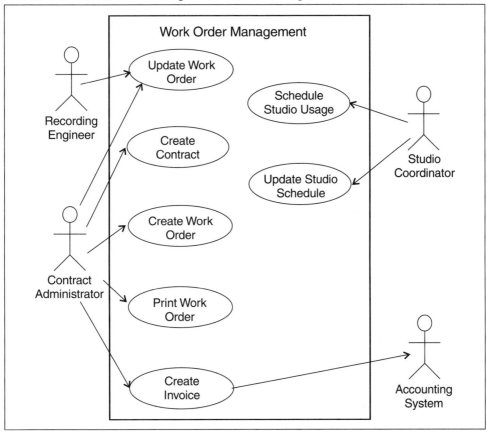

situations: to edit multiple video tapes onto one video tape or to produce live television programs. The company wanted to model the switch with use cases.

The first use case diagram they created looks like Exhibit 8-4. It seems reasonable that, except that we questioned whether the individual use cases were each a whole use case. They looked to us like steps in a larger process. Because each use case is small, all use cases are performed within a relatively short time period, and all the use cases are performed by the same person. The developers replied that if all these use cases are the steps of one larger use case, then they only have one use case for the entire system.

The first thing we considered was if there were other use cases for this system. There are two primary uses of the switch—one for editing video tapes and one for producing live broadcasts. We made those two different use cases. These use cases will have a lot in common, but there are significant differ-

Exhibit 8-3 Recording Studio Activity Diagram

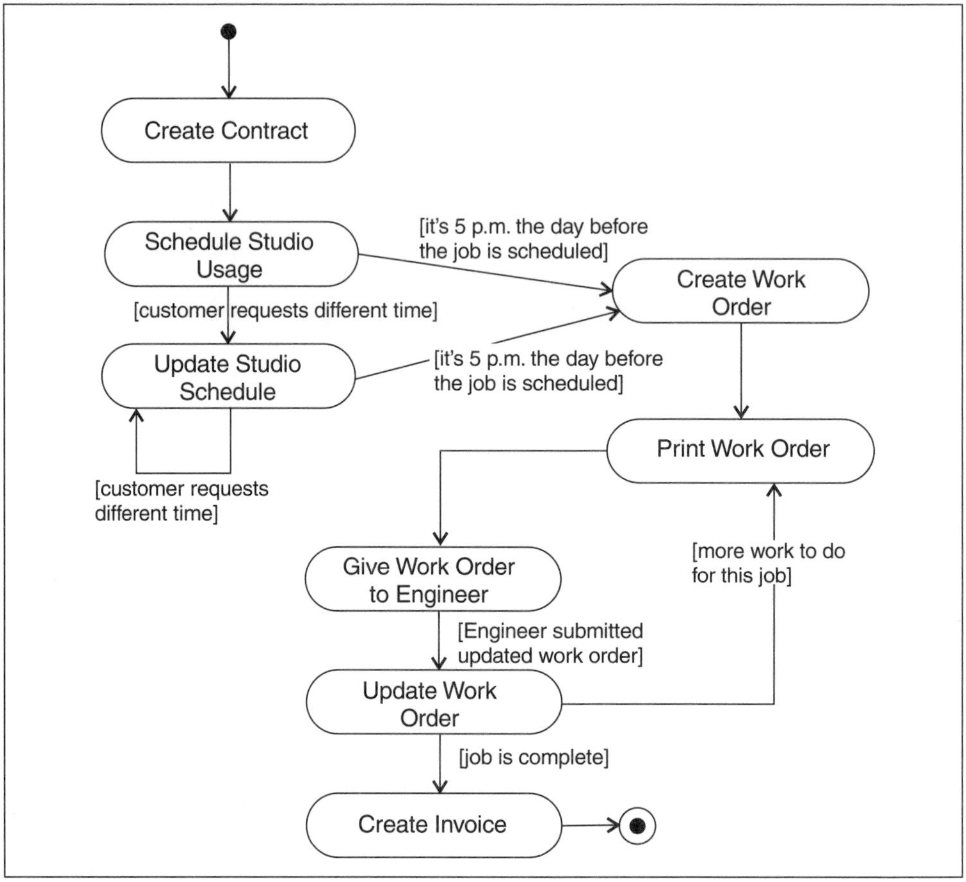

ences that need to be captured. Further questioning determined that there are two more use cases and another actor. The updated use case diagram is shown in Exhibit 8-5.

The developers had more questions. The old use cases are each a discrete step, but they have dependencies between them; some have to happen before others. This information is now a part of the Run a Live Program use case and would be in the text of that use case, but the developers wanted to show it on a diagram. So we created an activity diagram for the switch (see Exhibit 8-6), which shows nested activities. We needed a way to show that after a couple of initial steps are executed, the engineer can stop at any time. The activity Broadcasting encloses all the activities that can be interrupted by the engineer selecting end. At the bottom of the diagram, there is a transition from Broadcasting to the stop state. The transition happens on the event Engineer selects

Exhibit 8-4 Switch Use Case Diagram

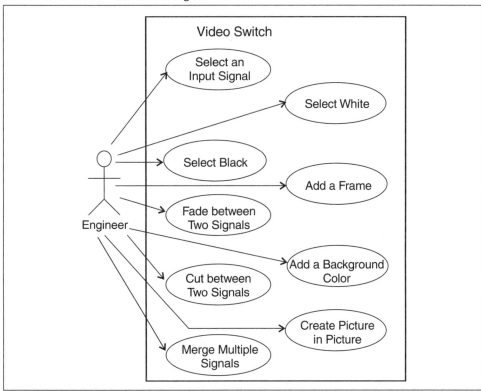

End. This is a way to show that the engineer can select End at any time after the Broadcasting activity has started and the use case stops.

If you think that you have only one use case for your entire system, consider a couple of possibilities. What is the level of detail for the use case? It is possible for an entire software project to be described by only one business process use case, because a business process use case describes a whole process from the point of view of someone outside your company. If you consider the Order Products business process use case for National Widgets, that one use case contains almost all of the functionality for the whole order-processing system, because, from the customer's point of view, everything the system does is part of getting the order to the customer.

If your one use case is already at the level of software, consider if your system is really that small. Some very small projects are truly just one use case. But also consider what you might be missing. In particular, consider if you need use cases for installation, shutdown, maintenance, and reporting. These are easy to miss when first creating use cases for a system.

Exhibit 8-5 Corrected Switch Use Case Diagram

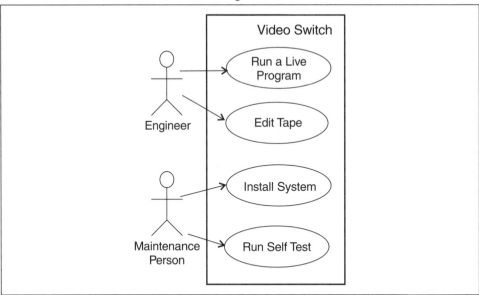

This example illustrates two main points. First, if one person performs a group of use cases within a relatively short time period, they may all be steps of one use case. Second, if you find only one use case for the whole system, consider the level of detail of the use case. This might be a business process use case for a small system, or you might not have found all the use cases. Determine if you need more use cases such as start up, shut down, or maintain the system.

Notice the difference between the recording studio example and the switch example. In the recording studio example there was a set of use cases that had to be performed in a particular order and different actors performed the use cases over a fairly large period of time. In that example the use cases were kept separate. In the switch example, there was a set of use cases that had to be performed in a particular order and the same actor performed them over a fairly short period of time. In that example the use cases were combined into one larger use case.

Screens as Use Cases

A company was creating an application that customers can use to apply for insurance. They designed all the screens first, then created one use case for each screen. Part of their use case diagram looks like Exhibit 8-7. We were

Exhibit 8-6 Run a Live Program Activity Diagram

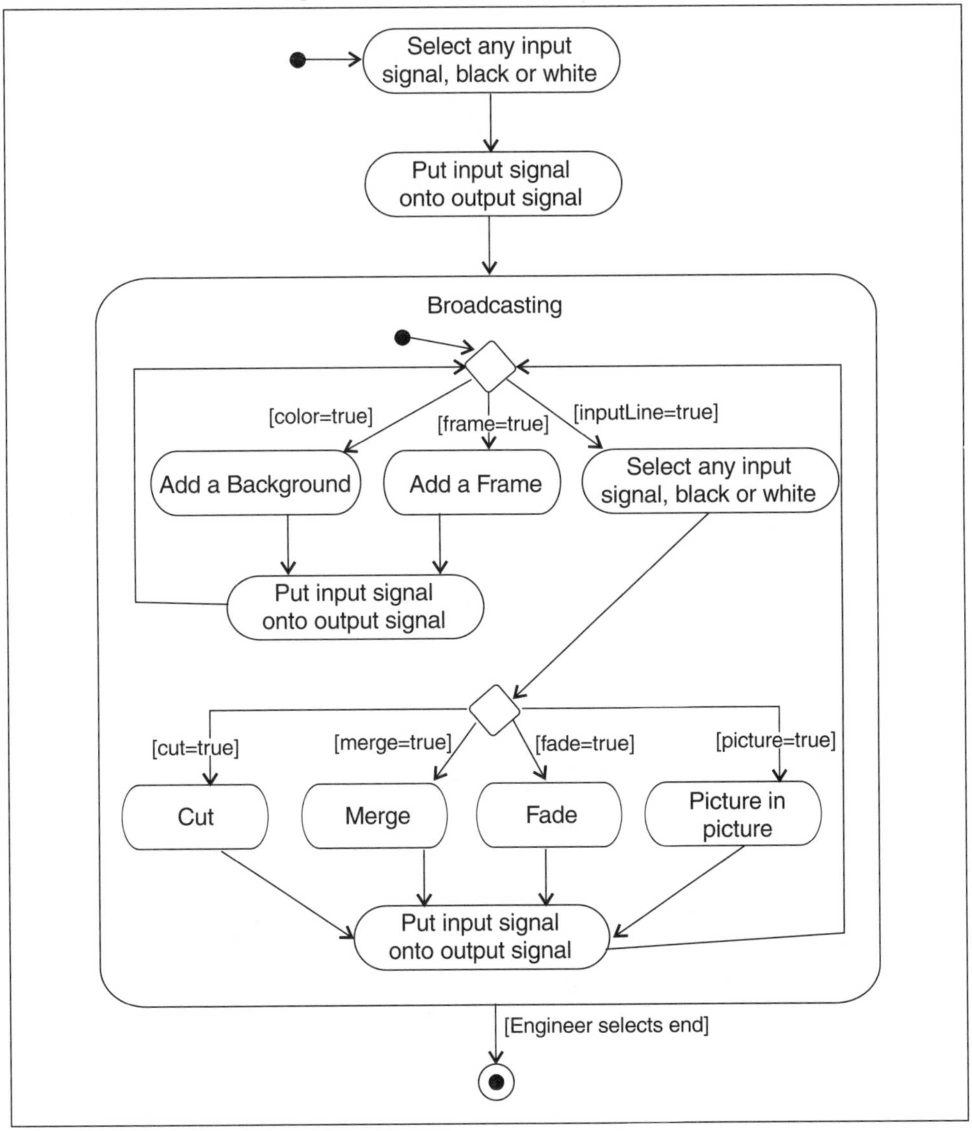

amazed. It had never occurred to us that someone would mutually include and extend between the same two use cases!

First we had to explain include and extend to the developers. If you consider the definition of include, it is not possible for two use cases to include each other. This would generate an infinite loop back and forth between the two. If you consider the definition of extend, it might be possible for two use cases to extend each other. You can avoid the infinite loop by care-

Exhibit 8-7 Insurance Application Use Case Diagram

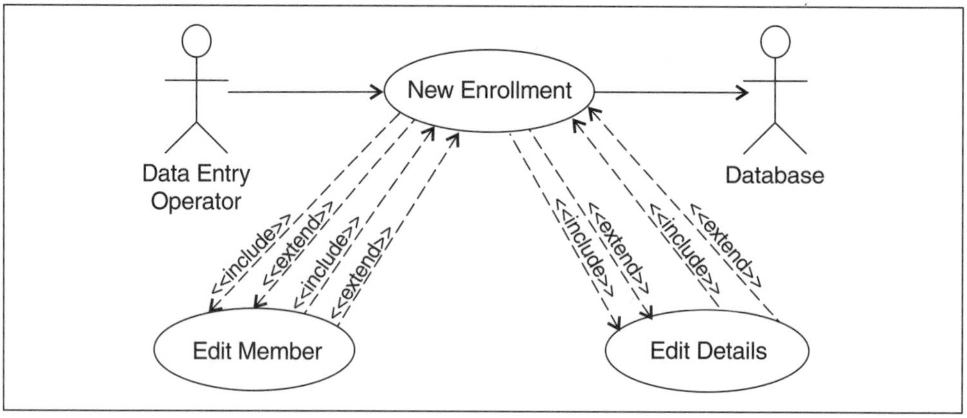

ful definition of the condition of the extend. However, this would be very confusing to understand and extremely error prone. So we recommend avoiding mutual extend and include completely.

After this discussion, the developers produced the use case diagram Exhibit 8-8. We questioned having both an include and an extend between the same two use cases. We had never come across a case where both were needed. The developers told us that they were using include and extend to express the same relationship. Since the relationship is not conditional, New Enrollment has to include Edit Member and Edit Details, so the right relationship is include, not extend.

But the developers had a problem with the new diagram, shown in Exhibit 8-9. They wanted to know how to show getting back to New Enrollment after Edit Member or Edit Details is finished. We explained that at the end of the included use case the return is automatic, but that wasn't what they meant. They wanted to know how to get back to the New Enrollment screen from the Edit Member or Edit Details screen. They had been using use cases to represent screens and include and extend relationships to show screen navigation.

We looked back at the text of the use cases and discovered that Edit Member and Edit Details are just steps of New Enrollment, not separate use cases at all. So the use case diagram really should look like Exhibit 8-10.

Remember that a use case is a complete task producing a result of value to an actor. One particular use case will very likely span several screens or pages in the user interface. Or a particular screen or page may be used by many use cases (think of a home page in a Web application where you can select many things to do). Screens are not use cases, and use cases are not screens.

Exhibit 8-8 Second Try at Insurance Application Use Case Diagram

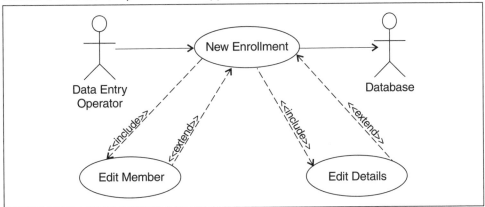

Exhibit 8-9 Corrected Insurance Application Use Case Diagram

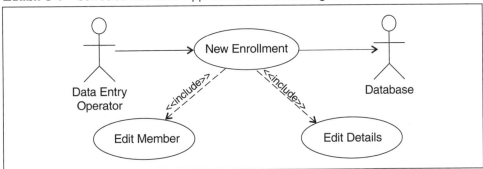

If you find two use cases mutually extending or including each other, ask what is intended. What is the diagram meant to represent? If the answer is navigation from one screen or page to another, this is the wrong relationship. Screen navigation is not shown on use case diagrams. Screen navigation will be documented with the user interface design. In general, you will not have two use cases mutually including or extending each other, nor will you have both an include and an extend relationship between the same two use cases.

Our experience is that it is better to write the use cases first, then design the screens and pages. This way, you avoid the problem.

Using Vague Terms

A company was creating an application that data entry operators can use to enter loan applications. Their first use case, which looks like Exhibit 8-11, is

Exhibit 8-10 Final Insurance Application Use Case Diagram

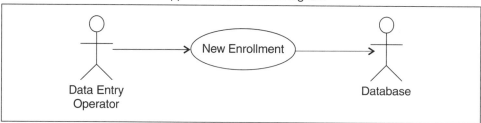

very high level, with a lot of vague terms. Our first question was, who is the intended audience?

We were told that this use case is meant for everyone from end users to developers. At this point, we had a lot of questions. An end user might ask what a required application field is or what an optional field is. A developer wants to know what happens when the application is submitted for processing. Is it just saved in the database, or is there additional work that the system has to do?

We suggested having two versions of this use case, one for the end user and one for the developer. The reason for this is that the end user really doesn't care about what happens when the loan application is processed. He or she is a data entry operator whose task is to enter loan application data quickly and efficiently. So the end user needs to know what has to be entered but not what happens to the application once it is submitted. On the other hand, the developer needs a lot more detail to be able to write the code for this use case.

Exhibit 8-11 Enter Loan Application

Basic Path

1. The use case begins when the Data Entry Operator selects Enter Loan Application.

2. The system displays a blank application form.

3. The Data Entry Operator completes all required application fields.

4. The Data Entry Operator opts to complete any optional fields.

5. The Data Entry Operator submits the application.

6. The system submits the data to the database for processing.

7. The system returns to the Loan Application screen, and the use case ends.

After this discussion, the business analysts produced a new version of the use case for the end user, shown in Exhibit 8-12. This use case includes only what the end user experiences when interacting with the system. Another version was produced for the developers, shown in Exhibit 8-13, that includes much more detail about the processing of the loan application—specifically, the complete business rules in order to produce the correct software for the system.

The two versions of the use case can be maintained in three ways. The first way we have shown as two separate use cases, which can be a problem when changes need to be made. Another way is to modify the end user version of the use case by adding a paragraph or nested steps showing the additional detail. See Exhibit 8-14 for an example using nested steps. Many word processing tools will let you hide sections of text. So if you want to produce a document for the end users, you can hide the nested steps with the additional detail. To produce a document for developers, show the nested steps.

A third way to handle multiple versions of a use case is with subordinate use cases. A subordinate use case is just a piece of another use case. It is

Exhibit 8-12   Enter Loan Application for Data Entry Operator

Basic Path

1. The use case begins when the Data Entry Operator selects Enter Loan Application.

2. The system displays a blank application form with the Application Date defaulted to the current date.

3. If the Application Date is not the current date, the Data Entry Operator will enter the correct Application Date.

4. The Data Entry Operator completes all required application fields, including Applicant Name, Applicant Address, Applicant Date of Birth, Employer Name, Employer Address, Yearly Income, Type of Loan, and Loan Amount Requested.

5. If there is a co-applicant, the Data Entry Operator completes the fields for Co-applicant Name, Co-applicant Date of Birth, Co-Applicant Employer Name, Co-Applicant Employer Address, and Co-Applicant Yearly Income.

6. If the co-applicant has a different address than the applicant, the Data Entry Operator completes the fields for Co-Applicant Address.

7. The Data Entry Operator submits the application.

8. The system clears the application form, and the use case ends.

Exhibit 8-13 Enter Loan Application for Developers

Basic Path

1. The use case begins when the Data Entry Operator selects Enter Loan Application.

2. The system displays a blank application form with the Application Date defaulted to the current date.

3. If the Application Date is not the current date, the Data Entry Operator enters the correct Application Date.

4. The Data Entry Operator completes all required application fields, including Applicant Name, Applicant Address, Applicant Date of Birth, Employer Name, Employer Address, Yearly Income, Type of Loan, and Loan Amount Requested.

5. If there is a co-applicant, the Data Entry Operator completes the fields for Co-Applicant Name, Co-Applicant Date of Birth, Co-Applicant Employer Name, Co-Applicant Employer Address, and Co-Applicant Yearly Income.

6. If the co-applicant has a different address than the applicant, the Data Entry Operator completes the fields for Co-Applicant Address.

7. The Data Entry Operator submits the application.

8. The system saves the application in the database.

9. The system clears the application form.

10. The system verifies that the applicant and co-applicant are at least 18 years of age.

11. The system generates a request to a credit bureau to get a credit check for the applicant and co-applicant.

12. The system generates a request to the applicant employer and co-applicant employer to verify employment and income.

13. The system calculates the debt ratio for the applicant and co-applicant, based on the report from the credit bureau and the verified income from the applicant employer and co-applicant employer.

14. The system calculates the amount of loan the applicant and co-applicant are allowed, based on the debt ratio.

15. The system verifies that the loan amount requested is less than or equal to the amount of loan allowed.

16. The system saves the results of the approval process.

17. The system generates a message to a sales representative with the results of the approval process, and the use case ends.

Exhibit 8-14 Enter Loan Application with Nested Steps

Basic Path

1. The use case begins when the Data Entry Operator selects Enter Loan Application.

2. The system displays a blank application form with the Application Date defaulted to the current date.

3. If the Application Date is not the current date, the Data Entry Operator enters the correct Application Date.

4. The Data Entry Operator completes all required application fields, including Applicant Name, Applicant Address, Applicant Date of Birth, Employer Name, Employer Address, Yearly Income, Type of Loan, and Loan Amount Requested.

5. If there is a co-applicant, the Data Entry Operator completes the fields for Co-Applicant Name, Co-Applicant Date of Birth, Co-Applicant Employer Name, Co-Applicant Employer Address, and Co-Applicant Yearly Income.

6. If the co-applicant has a different address than the applicant, the Data Entry Operator completes the fields for Co-Applicant Address.

7. The Data Entry Operator submits the application.

    7.1 The system saves the application in the database.

8. The system clears the application form.

    8.1 The system verifies that the applicant and co-applicant are at least 18 years of age.

    8.2 The system generates a request to a credit bureau to get a credit check for the applicant and co-applicant.

    8.3 The system generates a request to the applicant employer and co-applicant employer to verify employment and income.

    8.4 The system calculates the debt ratio for the applicant and co-applicant, based on the report from the credit bureau and the verified income from the applicant employer and co-applicant employer.

    8.5 The system calculates the amount of loan the applicant and co-applicant are allowed, based on the debt ratio.

    8.6 The system verifies that the loan amount requested is less than or equal to the amount of loan allowed.

    8.7 The system saves the results of the approval process.

    8.8 The system generates a message to a sales representative with the results of the approval process.

9. The use case ends.

extracted from the main use case and written separately. This is commonly done to add more detail to an existing use case when you don't want the details in the main use case. See Exhibit 8-15 for an example of using a subordinate use case to add detail.

If you find a use case with vague terminology, determine the intended audience to see if the level of detail is appropriate. If more detail is needed, is it needed by every reader of the use case, or only some of them? If only some readers need the additional detail, consider how you will handle it. Will you maintain multiple versions of the same use case, use nested steps or paragraphs, or use subordinate use cases? Whatever method you choose, use it consistently throughout all of your use cases.

Business versus Technical Requirements

We are often asked about level of detail in requirements. The requirements of a system should tell what the system does, not how it does it. This means that there should be no design information in the system requirements. It is very common for design information to creep into the requirements. We have included here a commonly seen requirement that is a design decision masquerading as a business requirement: The system will support a Web browser interface. This is a particular design for a user interface. We need to find out the actual requirements behind that design decision.

When we see this kind of requirement, we start asking questions. The obvious question here is: Why do you require a Web browser interface? One answer you may get is: Because that's what users want. That still isn't a requirement, so ask another question: What do the users like about a Web browser interface. Perhaps you will get an answer such as: The users like a Web browser interface because it is comfortable, easy to use, and they don't have to learn something new. Now you have requirements. You will want to refine the answer further to quantify what is meant by comfortable and easy to use. Does that mean easy for anyone or easy for a power user? How will you measure easy to use? These questions will lead to requirements that are testable.

You may still build the system with a Web browser interface, or you may decide that another kind of interface meets the users needs better. Now you know what the users actually need, so you can build a system that meets their actual requirements.

If you see a requirement that tells how the system should be designed or constructed, ask questions to find out the actual requirements behind that design decision. Those requirements will be important to the success of your project.

Exhibit 8-15   Enter Loan Application with Subordinate Use Case

Basic Path

1. The use case begins when the Data Entry Operator selects Enter Loan Application.

2. The system displays a blank application form with the Application Date defaulted to the current date.

3. If the Application Date is not the current date, the Data Entry Operator enters the correct Application Date.

4. The Data Entry Operator completes all required application fields, including Applicant Name, Applicant Address, Applicant Date of Birth, Employer Name, Employer Address, Yearly Income, Type of Loan, and Loan Amount Requested.

5. If there is a co-applicant, the Data Entry Operator completes the fields for Co-Applicant Name, Co-Applicant Date of Birth, Co-Applicant Employer Name, Co-Applicant Employer Address, and Co-Applicant Yearly Income.

6. If the co-applicant has a different address than the applicant, the Data Entry Operator completes the fields for Co-Applicant Address.

7. The Data Entry Operator submits the application.

8. The system clears the application form. See subordinate use case Application Processing Business Rules for more detail.

9. The use case ends.

Subordinate Use Case: Application Processing Business Rules

1. The system saves the application in the database

2. The system verifies that the applicant and co-applicant are at least 18 years of age.

3. The system generates a request to a credit bureau to get a credit check for the applicant and co-applicant.

4. The system generates a request to the applicant employer and co-applicant employer to verify employment and income.

5. The system calculates the debt ratio for the applicant and co-applicant, based on the report from the credit bureau and the verified income from the applicant employer and co-applicant employer.

6. The system calculates the amount of loan the applicant and co-applicant are allowed, based on the debt ratio.

7. The system verifies that the loan amount requested is less than or equal to the amount of loan allowed.

8. The system saves the results of the approval process.

9. The system generates a message to a sales representative with the results of the approval process.

CHAPTER REVIEW

In this chapter we considered various ways of looking at a project, including technical, user, market, and the needs of the future. We also revised use cases for commonly made mistakes and corrected them. Although we only talk about reviews in this chapter, they are something that should be applied during every phase of the project. By now you should understand your system very well and be ready to build it.

Table 8-1 lists the elaboration phase deliverables that should be complete. In the next chapter we will look at mechanisms for taking projects that are large and complex and breaking them into smaller pieces that are easier to work with.

Table 8-1 Elaboration Phase Deliverables

Complete	Deliverables
✔	Detailed basic path
✔	Alternative paths
✔	Activity diagrams
✔	User interface diagrammed (optional)
	Architecture
	Project plan

Chapter 9

Dividing Large Systems

What if you have been going through the process and you find that you need more detail—everything is too high level, too abstract? It may be that your use cases are not detailed enough. But it's also possible that your system is too big to deal with altogether. If so, you need an approach to break the system into pieces that are small enough to work with.

We will start by defining the modules of the architecture of the system. An architecture is specific to a particular application, but we'll go through a few basic architectural patterns in this chapter to give you some ideas. These patterns provide a basic framework for the system without going into detail about the contents of the system. You may find that several of the patterns can be applied to your project. Because software architecture is beyond the scope of this book, we have listed some good books on it in Appendix A.

After considering architectures, we'll look at how to divide use cases between the modules of the architecture. We have to consider what to do about actors and how to trace from a high-level system use case to its parts in the various modules of the system.

ARCHITECTURAL PATTERNS

 While reading the previous chapters, you may have found yourself identifying significant parts of your system. Or you may have a requirement to develop your system as a three-tier architecture. Or you know your system must be distributed. You would like to capture that information somewhere. The first step is to consider various patterns of architectures and pick one that looks like it fits your system. Then go on to add details to the pattern, such as contents of the modules and interfaces between the modules. As you fill in the details, it will become clearer whether or not the pattern actually fits.

An architectural pattern is a generalized overview of the structure of some set of systems. Each pattern is very general so that it applies to a broad range of systems. Looking over architectural patterns will give you a better view into the problem you are trying to solve. It also may be useful in determining the feasibility of one or more parts of the system being developed.

Start by picking out the major pieces of your system. These should be things that jump out at you. We will present an example for the order-processing software that uses a piece that handles order taking, a piece that processes payments, and a piece that handles order shipping. These pieces are represented by UML subsystems.

Next, write descriptions of your subsystems. This will help you determine whether the subsystems are well defined and will help you find the interfaces between the subsystems—that is, which subsystems work with which other subsystems? Finally, as you determine the patterns of relationships, you will want to try matching your subsystems and relationships to some architectural patterns.

We'll look at several architectural patterns and then examine the process in more detail for the order-processing software. See Appendix A for books on software architecture and architectural patterns.

Three-Tier Architectural Pattern

We will start by looking at a simple three-tier architectural pattern. In this pattern, one tier holds the user interface, one holds the business rules, and one holds the database. Exhibit 9-1 graphs this using subsystem packages from the UML notation. The arrows show a dependency relationship. For example, for Business Rules to do its job, it needs something from Database.

Where do the pieces of the order-processing software fit in? Each one will be split between the tiers. For example, look at order taking. The form used to record the order will be a part of the User Interface tier. The data collected for the order will be in the Database tier. The process used for taking an order will be in the Business Rules tier. The other parts will be similarly divided.

Exhibit 9-1 Three-Tier Architecture Example

This kind of approach can be good if the goals of your system include having a consistent look across all functions, having one database used by everyone, and having a consistent set of business processes. Alternatively, you may decide to start out by buying an order-processing system that is structured as a user interface, a set of business processes, and database. All you need to do then is modify the pieces of this software to fit your particular needs.

Pipe and Filter Architectural Pattern

A very different type of pattern is the pipe and filter. The basic idea of a pipe and filter pattern is that one piece inputs some data, transforms it somehow, and outputs it. The next piece then takes the information, transforms it somehow, outputs it, and so on. Each piece is independent and doesn't know about the other pieces.

What will this look like for our order-processing system? As shown in Exhibit 9-2, Take Orders does its function, then puts a stack of orders somewhere. Ship Orders picks up a stack of orders, fills, and ships them. Similarly, Process Payments picks up any payments and processes them. The graph of this pattern is different from the three-tier graph. Note that there are no dependency arrows between our subsystems. Each subsystem does its job completely independently of the others.

We can add and replace subsystems without changing the other subsystems. The only dependency is on the data, which we are showing here as a subsystem to illustrate the concept. The data might come from standard input and go to standard output. That would be the model for a traditional pipe and filter architecture, where the data is piped from one subsystem to another. Each subsystem reads data from standard input, filters or transforms it, and writes it to standard output. Instead of coming from standard input and going to standard output, the data can come from a file or database before it is transformed and written back out.

Exhibit 9-2 Pipe and Filter Architecture Example

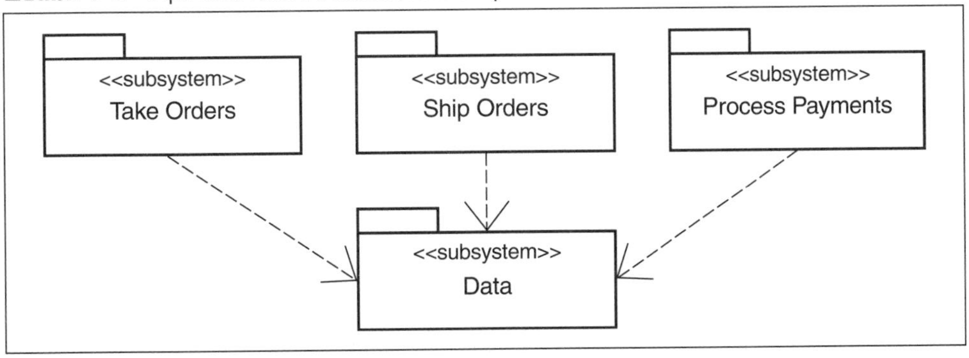

Pipe and filter is a good approach when you want the flexibility to add and delete subsystems at any time without having to change the others. Because the only dependency is on the data, it's easy to change a system when the change is adding or removing functionality.

Object-Oriented Architectural Pattern

For the last example (see Exhibit 9-3), we'll look at an object-oriented pattern. Here subsystems are defined around the data and its associated functions. The relationships are more flexible than in the other two patterns. Once identified, the subsystems can interrelate any way they need to in accomplishing the work of the system. In this example, Take Orders has dependencies on Ship Orders and Process Payments, but those subsystems don't know about each other. Take Orders contains orders and the functions that manipulate them. Process Payments deals with charges, credits, and accounts, and Ship Orders deals with packages and shipping information.

This approach emphasizes the dependencies between the pieces of the system while showing each function as a separate, self-contained piece. In contrast, in three-tier architecture, each function exists in three places—the user interface, business rules, and the database. In the pipe and filter architecture, the functions can relate only through the data.

Order-Processing Architecture Example

"Okay, Gus," Tara said. "Now that we have written down everything, we've found out a lot about our system. But we still don't have a good idea on how to turn this into something real! You explained about different types of architecture, but how do we know which one is right?"

Exhibit 9-3 Object-Oriented Architecture Example

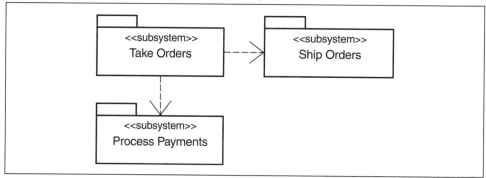

"Well, now we take what we can pull out of these lists and draw up our first attempt at an architecture for the order-processing software. Let's see . . . customers will submit orders, which we then fill and ship to them. Sounds like we need something for order input and also for shipping. And we have to have some way of processing payments. Okay, Let's put these into a chart." [See Exhibit 9-4.]

"Okay so far. But now we need to figure out how the pieces relate to each other."

"I think they are pretty independent," Lisa said. "One part just enters orders into the system. At another point in time, an order can have its payment information verified. Then, later, someone else could pull the order together and ship it."

"I see. So the only relationship so far between the parts is the orders themselves."

"Sounds kind of like it could be, oh, what was that called, Gus? The pipe and filter? Except I'd store the orders in a database somewhere rather than just pass them from part to part."

"Wait a minute," Dennis said. "We've been processing credit card payments as part of taking orders. Wouldn't that add a call between Take Orders and Process Payments?"

"We have to look at this more carefully because we have an inconsistency between our architecture and our process. Does that mean we have the wrong subsystems, the wrong architecture, or the wrong process? We have to change one of them, but what is the best change?"

"I like having all the payment processing stuff together," Lisa said. "No matter what kind of payment—credit card, check, money order—there will be similar things to do, so it makes sense to put them all together."

"I think I agree. The Process Payments subsystem seems reasonable. I don't want to split it up."

"What about including it inside Take Order?"

"No, because we need Return Product to do money-type things, too."

"Wait a minute. Where is Return Product? And how will Process Payments issue credits?"

Exhibit 9-4 Order-Processing Subsystems

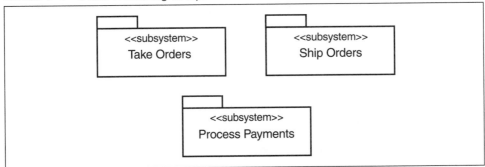

"Hold it!" Gus said, raising his hand. "Maybe our names are wrong. What if Process Payments is called Money Handling? Then it can have all the stuff about interfacing to the accounting system, updating accounts, charging and crediting customers, handling checks, credit cards, or money orders, and so on."

"Good. I like having the description of the subsystem. It makes it easier to figure out what is best."

"Ship Orders is still good," Tara continued. "That subsystem can interface with the inventory system to find the parts of the order; then it can generate a mailing label and calculate shipping and handling for the order. All the things that go into actually packaging up and shipping an order."

"Sure. And that's independent of the rest of the system. We don't really care how we got the order or how many times it may have changed. It can just work off the database."

"So what about Take Orders? Do we need additional subsystems for Return Product and so on, or can we make a more general subsystem that manages the orders themselves?"

"Why not Manage Orders?" Lisa asked. "It can do all the order taking, returning of products, status of orders, and so on. It will write to the database, use information already in the database, and potentially make calls to Money Handling as well." [See Exhibit 9-5.]

"Will Money Handling use the Database?"

"I don't think so," Dennis replied. "I like the way it interfaces with the order management piece. It makes more sense to me. Let's try it that way for now."

"Hey," Lisa said. "Why aren't we showing our inventory and accounting systems?"

"Actually," Gus added, "because they're actors we don't include them here. This is a diagram of our system, and actors are always outside our system."

"It doesn't look like pipe and filter anymore."

Exhibit 9-5 Order-Processing Subsystems with Relationships

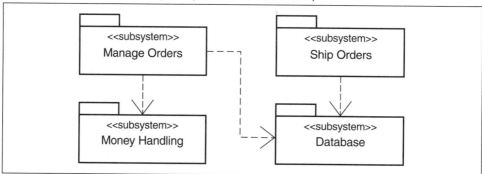

"No. I think we fixed our problem by changing the architecture and the subsystems and leaving the process alone. It looks more like an object-oriented architecture now."

"Hey, Gus, how do we know we got it right?"

TESTING THE ARCHITECTURE WITH USE CASES

At this point you have identified the basic subsystems for your system, written descriptions for them, identified relationships between them, and identified the basic architectural pattern you are using. But how do you know that what you have is right?

There are a couple of things you can do to test the architecture you have defined to see if it is correct and if it will work for your system. First, apply these tests to your subsystems to see if they are well defined as modules. Each subsystem should have

- A single functionality
- Strong (internal) cohesion—Its parts have a strong relationship to each other
- Loose (external) coupling—It doesn't depend too much on other subsystems to get its job done
- Minimal communication to other subsystems—The subsystems don't do much talking back and forth

Next, step through the architecture for each use case. For each step, determine which subsystem will handle that step. If one subsystem has to ask another subsystem to do part of the use case, is there a relationship between the two subsystems? Use this process to add to the descriptions of the subsystems, to add relationships between subsystems, to add descriptions to the relationships, and maybe even to add new subsystems. Let's look at the order-processing software for an example.

Gus and his friends have returned from dinner and continue where they left off.

"Lisa, you asked how we know if we got it right. That's a good question. Anyone?"

"Well," Dennis began, "if we could magically test it somehow . . ."

"That would be good, yes. Well, I can tell you how we can do some functional testing using the use cases we put together."

"Oh, good!" Tara said. "I was hoping to get more use out of those."

"Here's what we'll do. Let's take a use case," Gus said, rifling through the use case stack. "Let's start with Place Order. We'll step through it and assign each step to a subsystem. That will start to tell us who communicates with whom and what they will need to know."

Place Order Step 1

The use case starts when the customer selects Place Order.

Gus started the first one. "Who handles login and security?"

"It doesn't really fit anywhere currently defined, so I guess we need another subsystem."

"What do we call it?"

"What does it do?"

"It handles login and logout and checks for access permissions," responded Lisa. "We don't want customers to have access to our accounting system, for example."

"Well, let's call it System Access then," Gus said. "It will handle step one. Now what?"

Place Order Step 2

The customer enters his or her name and address.

"Sounds like something Manage Orders would do."

"How did we get there?" Gus asked.

Lisa looked puzzled. "What do you mean?"

"This is one use case. You can't start somewhere and appear somewhere else without going there from where you were. So how did we get there?"

"I guess System Access called Manage Orders to do the order taking."

"So we need an arrow between those subsystems. Next step."

Place Order Step 3

The customer enters product codes for products he or she wishes to order.

"Manage Orders does this. Next step."

Place Order Step 4

The system supplies a product description and price for each item.

"That sounds like something from the inventory system."

"But we don't have a subsystem for that because it's an actor."

"Our interface to it is from Ship Orders. Do we want to call Ship Orders to get product information?"

"That doesn't make sense," Tara said. "It's not a shipping function, although Ship Orders needs product information, too."

"Guess we need a subsystem that both Manage Orders and Ship Orders can use," Gus decided. "Let's call it Product Info. We call it to get all kinds of information about products. It can interface with the inventory system, and no one else has to know we are using an inventory system."

"So step four goes to Product Info with an arrow from Manage Orders to Product Info. Got it! Next step."

Place Order Step 5

The system keeps a running total of items ordered as they are entered.

"Manage Orders. Next."

Place Order Step 6

The customer enters credit card payment information.

"Manage Orders."

"Wait," Dennis said. "Shouldn't it be Money Handling?"

"No. We're just collecting information, not processing the payment."

"Oh, okay, Manage Orders. What's next?"

Place Order Step 7

The customer selects Submit.

"Manage Orders. Next."

Place Order Step 8

The system verifies the information, saves the order as pending, and forwards payment information to the accounting system.

"Verify Info looks like Manage Orders, but not the rest."

"Yeah. Database should do the save, and payment info goes to Money Handling."

Dennis smiles. "Sounds good to me. And we have those relationships in the diagram [see Exhibit 9-6] already. Next step."

Place Order Step 9

When payment is confirmed, the order is marked confirmed, an order ID is returned to the customer, and the use case ends.

Exhibit 9-6 Order-Processing Subsystems Updated

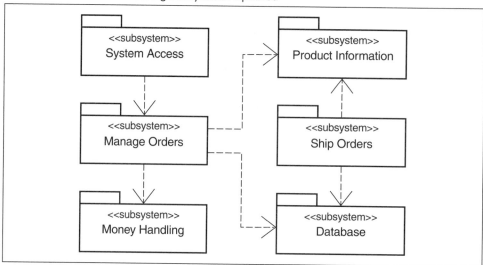

"Okay. So we know payment confirmation is Money Handling from the previous step. The rest looks like Manage Orders."

"But we change the status of the order so that it will require the Database to update it."

"Okay. And who generates the order ID?"

"Probably Database because it knows how many are already entered."

"Yeah, but so does Manage Orders, and I think the function fits better there. Database should just be store, retrieve, and update-type functions."

"Hmm. I agree. The order ID can go in Manage Orders. Let's see what we have now, and while we're at it, let's write a description for each subsystem."

System Access Subsystem

This subsystem handles login and logout, and checks for access permissions.

Product Info Subsystem

This subsystem provides information about products. It interfaces with the inventory system.

Manage Orders Subsystem

This subsystem handles order taking, product return, status of orders, and order canceling.

Ship Orders Subsystem

This subsystem prints pick lists for orders, generates mailing labels, and calculates shipping and handling for orders.

Money Handling Subsystem

This subsystem interfaces to the accounting system, updates accounts, charges and credits customers, and handles checks, credit cards, or money orders.

Database Subsystem

This subsystem contains the data we need to store for the application. It provides standard store, retrieve, update, and delete functions for the data stored.

SEQUENCE DIAGRAMS

The information in the exercise just completed can be captured in a sequence diagram. We can represent actors and subsystems in a sequence diagram and show the behavior of the systems as messages between the subsystems. Place Order is diagrammed in Exhibit 9-7, showing the interactions between subsystems. Compare Exhibit 9-7 to the exercise of assigning use case behavior to subsystems in the dialogue section above. The exercise and the diagram provide the same information in different forms.

This is another application of the sequence diagrams that we first saw in Chapter 5. Compare Exhibit 9-7 with Exhibit 5-8. Here the system object has been replaced with subsystems, which in a sequence diagram are represented by components. The actors and messages remain the same. Messages to the system become messages to particular subsystems. Messages that go from the system to itself become messages between subsystems.

DEFINING INTERFACES BETWEEN SUBSYSTEMS

In the previous section, we found operations that one subsystem called in another subsystem. We drew an arrow to show that a relationship existed, but now we also need to record what the actual operations are. In the UML we add interfaces to the subsystems to show the operations they implement. These are the same interfaces described in Chapter 4, but now we apply them to subsystems.

In this section, we introduce a new notation for interfaces. In Chapter 4 we defined the interface in text (see Exhibits 4-20 and 4-22), then put the interface on the use case diagram as a circle with a name below it (see Exhibit 4-23).

Exhibit 9-7 Sequence Diagram for Place Order using Subsystems

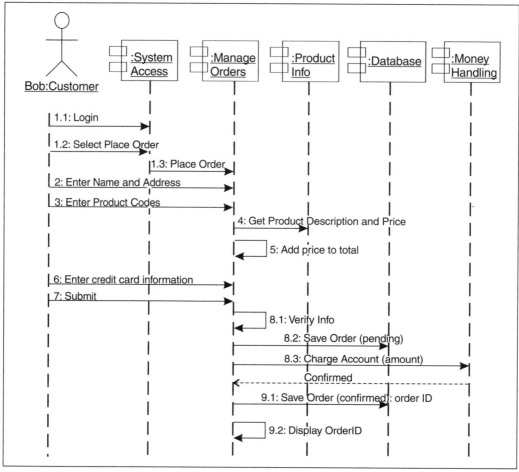

This is called the lollipop notation because it looks like a round lollipop on a stick.

Now we will put all the information on one diagram (see Exhibit 9-8). The interface is a rectangle with the word "interface" at the top followed by the interface name. In the compartment below is a list of the operations of the interface. The arrow marked <<realizes>> means that a subsystem has to provide an implementation for the interface. For example, in Exhibit 9-8 the Manage Orders subsystem realizes the IManageOrders interface. That means the Manage Orders subsystem has to supply code to implement the operations in that interface. The other dashed arrow shows who uses the interface. For example, in Exhibit 9-8 the System Access subsystem uses the IManageOrders interface, which means that the subsystem can use the operations in that interface.

Exhibit 9-8   Order Processing with Interfaces

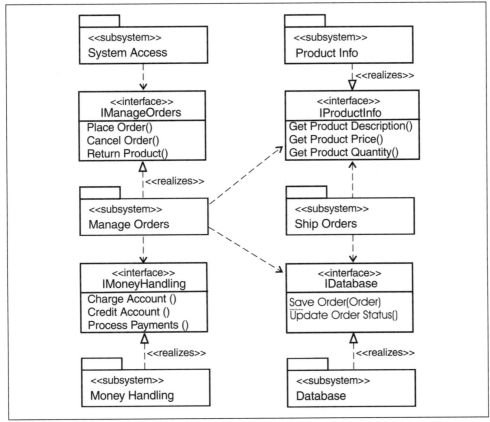

The operations in the interface come from the sequence diagram. Messages to the subsystem become operations in the interface. Some of the subsystems don't have interfaces. Notice that these subsystems are not called by any other subsystem. As we go through all the use cases, however, we may find occasions when we need to make calls to System Access or Ship Orders, or when an actor calls those subsystems. If so, we will add interfaces to those subsystems. The other subsystems have interfaces with some operations listed in them. For example, for Manage Orders, the interface shows the operations Place Order, Cancel Order, and Return Product because other subsystems expect Manage Orders to supply those operations.

Right now all we have are names. In some cases, we may need to send data to the subsystem along with the operation. In the Database subsystem, for example, we send along the order to be saved. Eventually all the operations will be updated to show what data is passed with them, if any. We will continue adding operations to the interfaces as we go through all the use cases in the system.

Look again at Exhibit 9-8 and notice that no arrows point to the subsystems. It is very easy to replace one subsystem with another subsystem in this example. As long as the new subsystem implements all the operations in the interface it realizes, nothing else in the system will know that the subsystem has been replaced. The ability to easily replace one subsystem with another is the primary advantage of using interfaces with subsystems.

"Now that we have identified some of the subsystems, let's write out our interfaces with them."

"Wait!" Tara said. "I think I know what you mean. You're telling us to write down what each of these subsystems should be telling the others when they do the work. For example, when we pass a customer order from the Manage Orders subsystem over to the Database subsystem, we have to tell Database which order and what to do with it. That's the definition of the interface—what we tell them, as well as the fact that we tell them."

"Exactly! And by writing it down, we solidify our design just a little bit more."

"How do we know our interfaces are complete?"

"We don't right now. The idea here is to put down what we know now and add to it later as we come across it, remember? That's how this keeps growing. Every time we learn something new, we add it in, and that tells us more about it."

SUBORDINATE USE CASES

One rule of use cases is that any particular use case must be contained completely in one system or subsystem. Now that we have subsystems defined, we need to divide the system-level use cases into subsystem-level use cases. We'll use the same sort of step-by-step process of going through the use cases, but now the purpose is to create new use cases that are subordinates of the system-level use cases. This is another use of the subordinate use cases discussed in Chapter 8 (see Exhibit 8-15).

We have already looked at each step of our use cases and have allocated them to some subsystem of our architecture. That subsystem is responsible for handling that step, which becomes a use case for that subsystem. The new use case is at the subsystem-level—a subordinate of the original system-level use case of which it was a step. You also might combine several steps of a system-level use case into one subordinate use case. Or you might split one step from a system-level use case into several subordinate use cases.

Let's look at an example using the Place Order use case. Place Order is a system-level use case for our order-processing software. It is also called a superordinate use case because it has subordinate use cases. Exhibit 9-9 shows the original Place Order use case.

Place Order fits mostly within the Manage Orders subsystem. So we'll allocate it to that subsystem and examine the steps to see what doesn't fit in Manage Orders. Those steps will become subordinate use cases in other subsystems. We said that step 1 would be handled by System Access, so it is a subordinate use case of that subsystem. We'll reword it a little to make it more general purpose.

Log in Subordinate Use Case

The user logs in to the system and selects an activity from some offered set of activities.

Steps 2 and 3 are handled by the Manage Orders subsystem, so we don't need to separate them out. Step 4 is handled by Product Info, so that will go in a separate use case.

Get Product Description and Price Subordinate Use Case

The system supplies a product description and price for each item.

Steps 5 through 7 and verifying information will stay in Manage Orders, so we don't separate them out. In step 8, "saves the order as pending" is clearly handled by the Database subsystem.

Save Order Subordinate Use Case

The system saves the order.

Step 9 also becomes more than one subordinate use case. Validating payment information goes to Money Handling, and Update Order Status is another call to the Database subsystem. The Place Order use case can be updated to show the changes, as seen in Exhibit 9-10.

Validate Payment Subordinate Use Case

The system validates the payment.

Update Order Status Subordinate Use Case

The system updates the order status.

Exhibit 9-9 Place Order Superordinate Use Case

1. The use case begins when the customer selects Place Order.

2. The customer enters his or her name and address.

3. If the customer enters only the zip code, the system supplies the city and state.

4. While the customer enters product codes
   a) The system supplies a product description and price.
   b) The system adds the price of the item to the total.

end loop

5. The customer enters credit card payment information.

6. The customer selects Submit.

7. The system verifies the information, saves the order as pending, and forwards payment information to the accounting system.

8. When payment is confirmed, the order is marked confirmed, an order ID is returned to the customer, and the use case ends.

Once all the use cases have been distributed, look at the actors for the system. Each actor will need to interface with some subsystems in the architecture. Determine which subsystems to associate with the actor. You also will have new actors in your system because each subsystem now becomes an actor to the other subsystems. We will find interactions with the subsystem actors when we add details to the new use cases.

What are the relationships between these subordinate use cases? A use case by definition must execute completely within a module. Include and extend do not go across module boundaries. This was no problem for our system-level use cases because the whole system was the module. But now our module is one subsystem. The use cases for that subsystem must execute completely within that subsystem. Because the subordinate use cases are in different subsystems and each subsystem is an actor to the others, the relationships between these subordinate use cases are implemented by communicates associations as shown in Exhibit 9-11.

Are there any requirements that were not satisfied by the system-level use cases? These might be internal processes that are not visible to actors at the system level. If you can make one of these internal requirements into a use case, go ahead and do that. Then allocate the new use case to one of your subsystems. You may find you need to add one or more new subsystems to accommodate these internal requirements.

Exhibit 9-10   Place Order Use Case Updated

Flow of Events

Basic Path

1. The use case begins when the customer logs in to the system and selects Place Order (Subordinate use case Log in).

2. The customer enters his or her name and address.

3. If the customer enters only the zip code, the system supplies the city and state.

4. While the customer enters product codes

    a) The system supplies a product description and price (Subordinate use case Get Product Description and Price).

    b) The system adds the price of the item to the total.

end loop

5. The customer enters credit card payment information.

6. The customer selects Submit.

7. The system verifies the information.

8. The system saves the order as pending (Subordinate use case Save Order).

9. The system forwards payment information to the accounting system (Subordinate use case Validate Payment).

10. The system marks the order confirmed (Subordinate use case Update Order Status).

11. The system returns an order ID to the customer, and the use case ends.

Subordinate Use Cases

Log in

The user logs in to the system and selects an activity from some offered set of activities.

Get Product Description and Price

The system supplies a product description and price for each item.

Save Order

The system saves the order.

Validate Payment

The system validates the payment.

Subordinate Use Case Update Order Status

The system updates the order status.

Exhibit 9-11 Updated Use Case Relationships

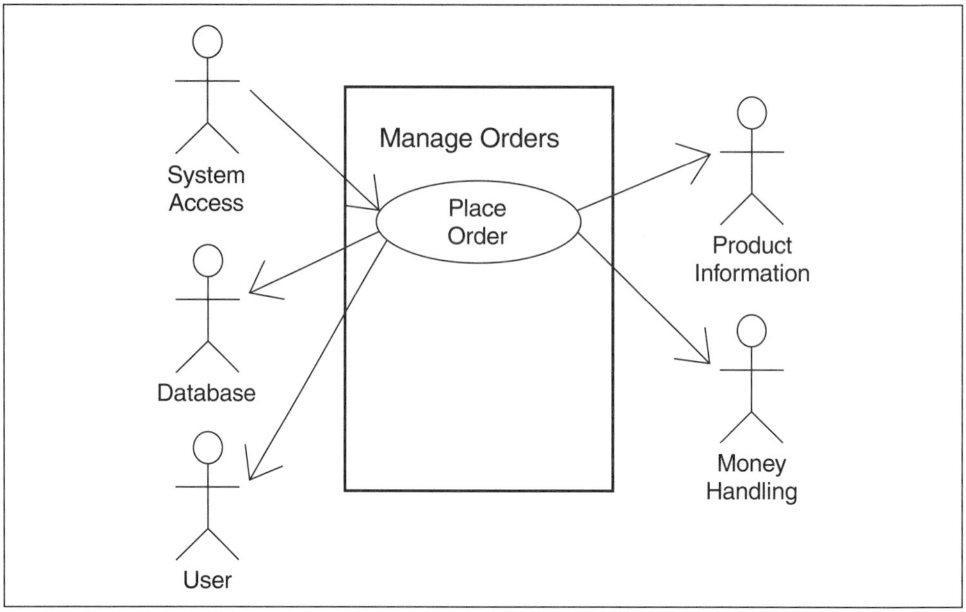

CREATING SUBSYSTEM DOCUMENTATION

At this point, you can treat each subsystem as if it were a whole system. Each one has actors and use cases, so you can create a use case diagram for each subsystem. The new use cases will need descriptions. The whole process as described in this book will be applied iteratively to each subsystem.

Let's look at a use case diagram for a subsystem we have defined using a new use case we found for Place Order (see Exhibits 9-12 and 9-13). We are adding arrows to the communicates relationship between actor and use case to indicate the direction of communication. Thus, the user starts the Log In use case, which sometime in that process, contacts the Manage Orders subsystem actor to start the Place Order use case. At this point, we move over to the use case diagram for Manage Orders (see Exhibit 9-11). In this subsystem, Place Order executes, using relationships to other subsystem actors to do its job.

We also want to detail the steps of each of the subordinate use cases, as we did for the system-level use cases. This use case can have alternative paths, activity diagrams, and a storyboard for the user interface. Each new subsystem can have an architecture, so we treat each subsystem as a complete system. You would do similar documentation for all the new subsystems you have defined.

Exhibit 9-12 System Access Use Cases

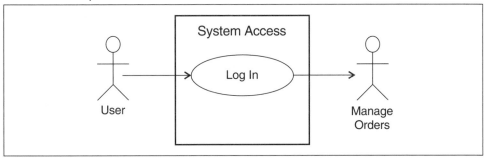

Exhibit 9-13 Log In Subordinate Use Case

1. The use case begins when the user starts the login function.

2. The user enters a username and password.

3. The system verifies the username and password.

4. The system sets access levels for the user.

5. The user selects an activity from a set of choices.

6. The activity is sent to Manage Orders.

7. The use case ends.

This process can be repeated for as many levels as you need to define your system. Eventually you will reach a point where a subsystem is small enough so that you have enough detail to implement it without further dividing it. If you get to a point where you are calling one class a subsystem, you have gone too far!

In Appendix E you will find all the use cases and subsystems for the National Widgets Order-Processing System.

SUBORDINATE VERSUS ALTERNATIVE VERSUS INCLUDE

Subordinate use cases look very similar to alternative flows of events and included use cases. So when do we use one or the other? A subordinate use case is part of another use case. It is documented in the same document as the use case it is part of, and it is used only by that use case. The superordinate use case is not complete without the subordinate use case. An alternative flow of events is a different way of executing a use case. There is at least one complete scenario of the use case without the alternative. An included use case is separate, having its own documentation, and it is used by two or more other use cases. These other use cases are not complete without the included use case.

It is easy to convert a subordinate use case into an included use case. Suppose that you have a Submit Loan Application use case that has as a subordinate Enter Loan Information. As you write the Edit Loan Application you notice that it also needs Enter Loan Information. Thus, you remove Enter Loan Information from Submit Loan Application, and make it into a use case. Then you create one include relationship between Submit Loan Application and Enter Loan Information and create another between Edit Loan Application and Enter Loan Information.

CHAPTER REVIEW

In this chapter we have developed what is sometimes called a system of interconnected systems. This is because each subsystem of your system has become a whole system itself. These new systems have interfaces to each other. And taken together, they completely describe one higher-level system. We are most of the way through elaboration (see Table 9-1). The next chapter finishes elaboration by developing the project plan.

Table 9-1 Elaboration Phase Deliverables

Complete	Deliverables
✔	Detailed basic path
✔	Alternative paths
✔	Activity diagrams
✔	User interface diagrammed (optional)
✔	Architecture
	Project plan

Chapter 10

Use Cases and the Project Plan

Before we can build the system, we need a plan of attack. What will we work on first? How do we know something is complete? We will rely on use cases to develop the project plan for our system.

The final thing to develop in elaboration is the first project plan. Like our other documents, this will be updated over time to reflect knowledge gained as we work on the project. The primary documents we will use for this are the risk factors, market factors, list of assumptions, and all the use cases.

PLANNING THE PROJECT

The project plan will be based on iterations. An iteration is some piece of the project that can be analyzed, designed, coded, integrated, and tested. Each iteration produces working code, adding pieces to the system until the system is complete.

Using this approach, we integrate often, test often, and always have some amount of code that works. If a project gets to a point where it becomes obvious that some requirements will not be completed, there is always a working version that can be polished and delivered—the last complete iteration.

Start by determining how many iterations you will have in construction. For this, a couple of factors have to be taken into account. You have to consider the length of the project. In general you will have more iterations in longer projects. Also consider your company's environment. What is a comfortable amount of time for your team to go through a complete development cycle? Each iteration should be about the same length, perhaps two weeks, two months, or six months. You might determine the length of an iteration by planning the first one, and then estimating the time to build it. That will be the basic length of your iterations, which sets up a heartbeat for your project, a rhythm that your team will depend on. As you figure out what goes into each iteration, you may need to adjust the duration a bit, but all the iterations should be close to the same length.

Now you know how many iterations you will have and how long each one will be. Next you need to plan their contents. The prioritized list of risks is the key document for planning this. Make sure this list is up to date and the priorities are feasible. Also, be sure to consider assumptions and market factors when assigning priorities. These can be very important to the success of your project.

Now that you have a complete, prioritized list of risks for your project, look at those at the top. These are the risks that will cause project failure if they are not addressed. Look at the use cases and determine which ones handle the risks you have identified. These are the use cases you will implement in the first iteration in the construction phase. Repeat this process with the next-highest risks for the second iteration. Continue scheduling until you have filled up all your iterations with use cases to develop.

Very likely you will develop only some of the scenarios for a use case in any particular iteration. Other scenarios will be completed in other iterations. You want to find a piece of the system that will implement some complete piece of functionality, although not necessarily all of its alternatives and exceptions.

Some additional things besides risk must be considered when planning the project. Your first couple of iterations should implement the core functionality of your system. You want to include things like using a database, CORBA, or a network fairly early on. You might decide to build a simulator in the first iteration to represent items you won't have until later. For example, you may be building some software to control hardware. The hardware isn't built yet, so you create a simulator with the same interface that the hardware will have so that the software can be built and tested.

Frequently, the first iteration has fewer features and fewer scenarios implemented because you have to develop much of the supporting software. On the other hand, most of the work in the last iteration is adding new features. Adjust the work in each iteration to match the duration you decided on for it.

In this first planning stage, it is better to have more work planned in the first couple of iterations and let the last iteration be light on functionality. You will find more work as you go along, which will be added to the last iteration. You also may find that you have overestimated what you can accomplish, so you will end up moving work from an earlier iteration to a later one.

You will find it relatively easy to plan the first two iterations. The others will be more vague, which is okay. As you work through each iteration, you will get a better understanding of your system and your team and so will be able to update the plans for later iterations accordingly.

In addition to all the other planning, you will need to define the goal of the iteration. What are you trying to accomplish? How will you know if you have succeeded? Add this kind of information to your planning document.

Let's look at an example for our order-processing system.

"Hey, Gus, how much longer before we can start writing software?"

"Just as soon as we plan our approach to putting this system together."

"More documentation," Dennis muttered. "We're never going to get done unless we start!"

"Well, then, where would you start?" asked Gus, smiling at the others.

"Oh, I don't know. I've been thinking of the flow so long I forgot about the programming. Why don't we just pick a place and start writing code? I want to think I'm doing something!"

"Well, how about this? Why don't we list the use cases in their order of importance, then look at what we need to make the first one work?"

"Oh! I got it!" Lisa called out. "If we do that, then the most important parts are likely to be finished first because we have to have them working to finish the use case! That's great!"

"But how do we know which is the most important?" Tara asked. "Do we just pick the longest one and start there?"

"Actually, no. The longest one might not include the biggest risks."

"Oh! That's what you're going to do with that list! I wondered about that."

"Yes, that list is one of the things we'll use to decide which use case is most important. And for our first iteration, we want to cover the most important things."

"First iteration?" Dennis asked. "Why don't we just make a plan for the whole thing and start writing it?"

"Well, I can think of a very good reason right here. Why are we having this conversation?"

"Because I'm tired of just writing documents and want to get working! I want to see something actually get done!"

"Right! Getting something done is a great feeling. So, by breaking our system down into smaller steps, which we call iterations, we'll be able to write code and test it. We'll be able to see things get done."

"Oh. Instead of waiting until the whole project is done before we can see something tested and working, we can see pieces of it working now."

"Right! And each iteration gives us more confidence in our project because we'll use the riskiest use cases first. If they don't work, we can still change our use cases and architecture before we've wasted too much time. Here is our current list of use cases and our risk factors. What should we do first?

- Log In
- Place Order
- Return Product
- Get Product Information
- Update Account
- Update Product Quantities
- Cancel Order
- Find Order
- Get Status on Order
- Get Catalog
- Register Complaint
- Run Sales Report
- Receive Back Ordered Items
- Fill and Ship Order

Risk Factors

High:

- Some of the people designing the software are inexperienced.
- The system has to be easy for nontechnical people to use.
- Can we be successful if we don't support a Web interface?

Medium:

- How do we handle many simultaneous users in different parts of the company?

Low:

- How can we prevent lost orders on system failure?
- What if the system is immediately flooded with orders?
- How do we handle the database crashing?

"Well, Log In isn't important if we don't allow customers direct access. But I think we should do Place Order early so we have something in the database for the other use cases to use."

"That means we have to include Get Product Information and Update Account. And we will have coded the interfaces to both those other pieces of software. Sounds like plenty for a first iteration."

"I want to add Get Status on Order."

"Why?"

"Because Place Order just puts something into the database. I want to be able to get something back out to check it."

"Good idea."

"Hold on!" Gus exclaimed. "You are forgetting the risk factors. We have a high risk of project failure if we don't allow direct customer access through a Web interface, the system has to be easy to use, and we need time as a team to gain experience. I think you've defined a great second iteration, but we need something different for the first."

"Well, what do you suggest?" Lisa asked.

"We need to focus on the user interface. If we do Log In, and then design, code, and test the Web pages with a fake database, I think that is enough to get us started. That will get us all some experience with the tools and technologies; plus, we can show the Web pages to some nontechnical people we know and see what they think of it in terms of ease of use."

Iteration 1—Deadline Sept. 22

Goals for the Iteration:

We will have a well-designed, easy-to-use interface with the ability to control access to the system. The project team will be comfortable using the development tools and technologies.

- Log In, basic path only

Iteration 2—Deadline Nov. 1

Goals for the Iteration:

We will have the basics of ordering a product worked out, including the interfaces to the accounting and inventory systems. This will set up the framework of communication between all parts of our system, from the user interface to the other software systems and to the database.

- Order Product, basic path only
- Get Product Information, basic path only
- Update Account, basic path only
- Get Status on Order, basic path only

"Hey, why only basic path?"

"Because we have enough to do as it is. There is a bunch of stuff to work out so multiple people can use the system at the same time. What looks easy on the surface has a whole framework of software behind it that everything in our system will use. We'll do the alternatives in a later iteration, after we have the basic system working. What next?"

"Let's do Fill and Ship. It's the rest of the order cycle and lets us check that the product quantities are getting updated properly."

"Want to do the back-ordered stuff, too?"

"Sure."

Iteration 3—Deadline Dec. 1

Goals for the Iteration:

In this iteration we will implement the order-filling half of the process. This will complete the interfaces to the inventory system and will introduce an interface to the shipping companies.

- Fill and Ship Order, basic path
- Update Product Quantities, basic path
- Receive back-ordered Items, basic path

"Most of the rest is really easy now that we have the basic framework. The only one at all complicated is Return Product."

"Okay. Let's put it all into Iteration 4, and then add a final iteration for the alternatives."

Iteration 4—Deadline Jan. 1

Goals for the Iteration:

At the end of this iteration, we will have completed the basic paths. We will be ready to start taking and filling orders.

- Log In, basic path
- Return Product, basic path
- Cancel Order, basic path
- Find Order, basic path
- Get Catalog, basic path
- Register Complaint, basic path
- Run Sales Report, basic path

Iteration 5—Deadline Feb. 1

Goals for the Iteration:

At the end of this iteration, we will have completed the order-processing system.

- All alternative paths
- All error handling functionality

You can see that the later iterations include more functionality than the first one does. This allows the team to develop the basic mechanisms of the system first, with just a few functions to test it. Later iterations will depend on those mechanisms working. Some things you may need to develop early include error handling, interprocess communication, communication across networks, interfacing with a database, and transaction processing.

A benefit to this risk-driven, iterative approach becomes apparent in projects that cannot meet their final deadline. They will still be able to deliver a working system with the most important functionality in place, tested, and working. Features that cannot be included by the deadline can be planned for a later release of the product.

Build versus Buy Decisions

In planning the project, you need to consider if the team will build the whole system or if some components will be bought or reused. Perhaps some of the software is being developed by another company or by another division of your company.

Buying a piece of your system will save development time and may cost less than building it yourself. On the other hand, costs will be associated with integrating that software into your project. Some items you can buy include libraries of functions, databases and repositories; libraries of domain-specific elements; and special-purpose tools such as parsers, search engines, forms, spreadsheets, bug tracking systems, and so on. You also may be able to out-source work such as customer support, payroll, or order gathering.

"Hey, Lisa," Tara said, "how much time do you think it will take to write a database?"

"What? Hold it!" called Gus, leaning across the table. "Who said we're going to write a database?"

"Well, don't we have to? It's referenced here in the Place Order use case."

"We don't want to write a database! There are lots of them on the market. Let's just buy one."

"But wouldn't that mean that we're dependent on someone outside our company?"

"Yes, but I think that will be a smaller risk than writing one ourselves. If we pick the right database, we can get support from the manufacturer. Remember, our business is to take and fill orders. I'd rather spend time doing that than working on something we can buy. Besides, it'll be much faster."

"That's true," Dennis added. "If we purchase one, we just have to write the interface to it. That's got to be a lot faster than writing an entire database by ourselves, and we'd have to interface to it, anyway. Let's buy one. It seems the best route."

"But what happens if they go out of business? Do we have to start over?"

"Nope! Remember the operations we put in front of the database subsystem? Because we did that, the only thing that knows we have changed databases is the Database subsystem. None of our other software has to change! That's why we defined those subsystem operations early."

The risks associated with buying include the following:

- How reputable is the company you are buying from?
- How good are their systems?
- How long have they been in business?
- Who are their customers?
- If this company goes out of business, how hard will it be to replace this software with something new?
- Are there industry standards for the system you want to buy?
- Does a particular system adhere to these standards?
- How are you going to interface to this system? Do you need to add processes or software to implement the interface?
- How long will it take to learn to use the software?

Compare these risks to those of building the system yourself by asking the following questions:

- How good are my people?
- Do they have or can they learn the skills needed?
- Do we have enough time in the schedule to build this piece?
- Do we have enough money to build it?

If you decide to buy, include these risks in your project risk list and include the integration of purchased components in the project schedule.

Prototyping

You may want to build some prototypes during elaboration to try out some ideas or to determine if a high-risk feature is possible. These prototypes are not production-level code and may even be written in a language different from the one your project will use. Though you may decide to include pieces of the prototype in your project, they are essentially throw-away code.

As a result of the prototyping effort, you may decide that a certain feature is not feasible and so remove it. If that feature is critical, you may even decide to abandon the project. Better to make that decision now rather than after a couple of years of development.

You might decide that even though what you are trying to accomplish in the prototype is feasible, you will have to do it a different way. That may mean making changes to some or all of the documentation you have produced, including the project schedule.

ESTIMATING WORK WITH USE CASES

In 1993 Gustav Karner of Objectory AB, later acquired by Rational Software Corporation, researched how to estimate for a project based on use cases. His work was a modification of the research by Albrecht on function points. Karner's results were promising. We include his estimating method here for you to use as a starting point for determining the amount of work for your project. Our thanks to Rational Software Corporation for allowing us to include the research in this book.

Karner's method is preliminary and should be used with other estimating methods, such as function points or COCOMO, to get an idea of the number of man-months for your project. We are interested in hearing how well it works for you or what you would change to make it fit your projects better. We have included a response form in Appendix D.

Weighting Actors

Start the process by considering the actors for your system, determining whether each is simple, average, or complex. A simple actor represents another system with a defined application programming interface. An average actor is either another system that interacts through a protocol such as TCP/IP, or it is a person interacting through a text-based interface (such as an old ASCII terminal). A complex actor is a person interacting through a graphical user interface (see Table 10-1).

Count how many of each actor type you have. Then multiply each type by a weighting factor. The number of simple actors is multiplied by 1, the number of average actors by 2, and the number of complex actors by 3. Add these products together to get a total.

Table 10-1 Actor Weighting Factors

Actor Type	Description	Factor
Simple	Program interface	1
Average	Interactive, or protocol-driven, interface	2
Complex	Graphical interface	3

For our order-processing system, we find the following:
- Customer – complex
- Inventory System – simple
- Accounting System – simple
- Customer Service Manager – average
- Customer Rep – complex
- Clerk – complex
- Shipping Company – average

Table 10-1 indicates the following:

2 simple * 1 = 2
2 average * 2 = 4
3 complex * 3 = 9
Total actor weight for order processing: 2 + 4 + 9 = 15

Weighting Use Cases

Now do a similar process for the list of use cases. You don't need to consider included use cases or extending use cases. For each use case determine whether it is simple, average, or complex. The basis of this decision is the number of transactions in a use case, including alternative paths. For this purpose, a transaction is defined to be an atomic set of activities, which is either performed entirely or not at all. A simple use case has 3 or fewer transactions, an average use case has 4 to 7 transactions, and a complex use case has more than 7 transactions (see Table 10-2).

We haven't talked about classes yet, which are another mechanism for measuring use case complexity. If you already have picked out analysis classes for your system and determined which ones are used to implement a particular use case, you can use that information in place of transactions to determine use case complexity. We consider only analysis classes at this time, not those that we will add during design.

A simple use case can be implemented with fewer than 5 analysis classes, an average use case can be implemented with 5 to 10 analysis classes, and a complex use case can be implemented with more than 10 analysis classes

Table 10-2 Transaction-Based Weighting Factors

Use Case Type	Description	Factor
Simple	3 or fewer transactions	5
Average	4 to 7 transactions	10
Complex	More than 7 transactions	15

Table 10-3 Analysis Class-Based Weighting Factors

Use Case Type	Description	Factor
Simple	Fewer than 5 analysis classes	5
Average	5 to 10 analysis classes	10
Complex	More than 10 analysis classes	15

(see Table 10-3). We will look at classes and how they relate to use cases in Chapter 11.

Count how many of each type of use case you have. Then multiply each type by a weighting factor. The number of simple use cases is multiplied by 5, the number of average use cases by 10, and the number of complex use cases by 15. Add these products together to get a total.

For our order-processing system, we find the following:

- Place Order — average
- Return Product — average
- Cancel Order — simple
- Get Status on Order — simple
- Send Catalog — simple
- Run Sales Report — simple
- Register Complaint — simple
- Fill and Ship Order — average
- Back-Ordered Items Received — average

Using either Table 10-2 or Table 10-3, we find the following:

5 simple * 5 = 25
4 average * 10 = 40
0 complex * 15 = 0
Total use case weight for order processing: 25 + 40 + 0 = 65

Add the total for actors to the total for use cases to get the unadjusted use case points (UUCP). This raw number will be adjusted to reflect your project's complexity and the experience of the people on the project.

For order processing, we have

15 + 65 = 80 UUCP

Weighting Technical Factors

We have an idea of the complexity of the use cases and interfaces. Now we need to weight the UUCP for factors such as complexity of the project and experience level of the people on the project.

Start by calculating the technical complexity of the project. This is called the technical complexity factor (TCF). To calculate the TCF, go through Table 10-4 and rate each factor from 0 to 5. A rating of 0 means that the factor is irrelevant for this project; 5 means it is essential. Now, multiply each factor's rating by its weight from the table. Finally, add all these numbers together to get the total TFactors:

$$\text{TFactor} = \sum (\text{Tlevel}) * (\text{WeightingFactor})$$
$$\text{TCF} = 0.6 + (0.01 * \text{TFactor})$$

Let's rate the factors for National Widgets (see Table 10-5) and add all the extended values together:

$$0 + 3 + 5 + 1 + 0 + 2.5 + 2.5 + 0 + 3 + 5 + 3 + 5 + 0 = 30$$

Plugging that into our formula, we get

$$\text{TCF} = 0.6 + (0.01 * 30) = 0.9$$

Table 10-4 Technical Factors for System and Weights

Factor Number	Factor Description	Weight
T1	Distributed system	2
T2	Response or throughput performance objectives	1
T3	End-user efficiency (online)	1
T4	Complex internal processing	1
T5	Code must be reusable	1
T6	Easy to install	0.5
T7	Easy to use	0.5
T8	Portable	2
T9	Easy to change	1
T10	Concurrent	1
T11	Includes special security features	1
T12	Provides direct access for third parties	1
T13	Special user training facilities required	1

Table 10-5 National Widgets Numbers

Factor Number	Weight	Assigned Value	Extended Value	Reason
T1	2	0	0	Not planning on distributing first release
T2	1	3	3	Speed is likely limited by human input
T3	1	5	5	Needs to be efficient
T4	1	1	1	Easy processing
T5	1	0	0	Nice, but later
T6	0.5	5	2.5	Needs to be easy for non-technical people
T7	0.5	5	2.5	Needs to be easy for non-technical people
T8	2	0	0	Not at this time
T9	1	3	3	Sure
T10	1	5	5	Not exactly, but it is multiuser
T11	1	3	3	Simple security
T12	1	5	5	Customers
T13	1	0	0	So easy we don't need training

Now consider the experience level of the people on the project. This is called the environmental factor (EF). To calculate EF, go through Table 10-6 and rate each factor from 0 to 5. For factors F1 through F4, 0 means no experience in the subject, 5 means expert, 3 means average. For F5, 0 means no motivation for the project, 5 means high motivation, 3 means average. For F6, 0 means extremely unstable requirements, 5 means unchanging requirements, 3 means average. For F7, 0 means no part-time technical staff, 5 means all part-time technical staff, 3 means average. For F8, 0 means easy-to-use programming language, 5 means very difficult programming language, 3 means average.

Now multiply each factor's rating by its weight from the table. Finally, add all the numbers together to get the total F factors.

Table 10-6 Environmental Factors for Team and Weights

Factor Number	Factor Description	Weight
F1	Familiar with Rational Unified Process	1.5
F2	Application experience	0.5
F3	Object-oriented experience	1
F4	Lead analyst capability	0.5
F5	Motivation	1
F6	Stable requirements	2
F7	Part-time workers	−1
F8	Difficult programming language	−1

EFactor = $\sum$ (Flevel) * (WeightingFactor)
EF   = 1.4 + (−0.03 * EFactor)

Table 10-7 shows the ratings for National Widgets. We add all the extended values to get our EFactor:

1.5 + .5 + 1 + 2.5 + 5 + 10 + 0 + −2 = 18.5

Table 10-7 National Widgets Ratings

Factor Number	Weight	Assigned Values	Extended Values	Reason
F1	1.5	1	1.5	Most of team unfamiliar
F2	0.5	1	0.5	Most of team not programmers
F3	1	1	1	Most of team not programmers
F4	0.5	5	2.5	Gus is really good
F5	1	5	5	Team is really eager
F6	2	5	10	We don't expect changes
F7	−1	0	0	No part-timers
F8	−1	2	−2	We're looking at Visual Basic

Plugging that into our formula we get:

$$EF = 1.4 + (-0.03 * 18.5) = 0.845$$

Use Case Points

Finally, calculate use case points (UCP).

$$UCP = UUCP * TCF * EF$$

The use case points for National Widgets and the final estimation of time to complete the project is

$$UCP = 80 * 0.9 * 0.845 = 60.84$$

Project Estimate

At this point Karner suggests using a factor of 20 man-hours per UCP for a project estimate. But a close examination of his data leads us to suggest a refinement based on our experiences with customers. Go back and look at EF factors F1 through F8. Count how many of F1 through F6 are below 3 and how many in F7 and F8 are above 3. If the total is 2 or less, use 20 man-hours per UCP. If the total is 3 or 4, use 28. If the total is 5 or more, try very hard to change your project so that the numbers can be adjusted. Otherwise, your risk of failure will be quite high.

Why do we suggest these changes? The EF factors measure the experience level of your staff and the stability of your project. Any negatives in this area mean that you will have to spend time training people or fixing problems due to instability. The more negatives you have, the more time you will spend fixing problems and training people and the less time you will have to devote to your project.

Because we have three negative factors, we'll multiply by 28 man-hours per UCP to get 1,703.52 man-hours, which we'll round to 1,704. This gives us a little under 43 weeks at 40 hours a week, or most of a year for one person.

Because we have a small team of four people, we won't run into too many problems of communication or synchronization of effort. So we'll assume that they all work full-time, giving about 11 weeks of effort, and add 3 weeks for working out any team issues. (If you don't see why the 3 weeks were added onto the schedule, see Brooks, *The Mythical Man-Month*.) We should have our software up and running in about 14 weeks.

CHAPTER REVIEW

By now you should have a first project plan that details at least the first two iterations. You also might have used the use case point estimator, or some other method, to get an idea of the man-hours needed for this project (see Table 10-8).

We suggest that you try this estimator along with other project estimators you may already be using. The work is based on a small amount of research and needs to be fine-tuned with more input. If you try the estimator on your project, we would really like to hear from you. Let us know the ratings you used for the various factors and whether the results were close to the actual man-hours required to finish the project. We have even supplied a reply form in Appendix D.

The final chapter discusses use cases in the construction and transition phases of development.

Table 10-8 Elaboration Phase Deliverables

Complete	Deliverables
✔	Detailed basic path
✔	Alternative paths
✔	Activity diagrams
✔	User interface diagrammed (optional)
✔	Architecture
✔	Project plan

Chapter 11

Constructing and Delivering a System

We have spent a lot of time learning about our system and what we want it to do. Now we need to move forward and decide how we are going to construct the system. We'll start by identifying the key abstractions in the system. Then we'll show how the key abstractions relate to the use cases, architecture, and project plan. The rest of our construction activities center around an iteration. We will look at planning, testing, and reviewing the iteration, using the documents we have previously written. Finally, we will consider the uses of use cases when preparing the product for market and beyond.

KEY ABSTRACTIONS OF THE DOMAIN

We'll start by identifying key abstractions. Key abstractions are things that are important and meaningful in your system. They are the primary things you work with in creating your system. They are the words you use to describe your domain.

The domain is the subject area you are working in. Some examples of domains are mail order companies, satellite communications, voice messaging, accounting, machine controllers, hospital administration, and library management. Within a domain, your project is solving a particular problem. Both the domain and the problem have a vocabulary to describe them. That vocabulary expresses the key abstractions of your system.

"Okay, Gus. How do we go from use cases to software?"

"We need to find key abstractions and detail what they mean."

"What's a key abstraction?"

"Key abstractions are the things we use in our order-processing system."

"Would that be like a computer? Or Gus?" Lisa asked.

"No!" Gus laughed. "No, nothing like that. It would be our products and the order forms we fill out. Those would be key abstractions."

"So a key abstraction is something that gets used or manipulated in our use cases? Okay, I can understand that. So, how do we find them?"

Identifying Key Abstractions in Use Cases

Some of the key abstractions are obvious; these are the things that you use in creating a system in a particular domain. For example, in an order-processing system, we know that we are going to be dealing with orders. However, others won't be as obvious.

There are other ways to find the initial key abstractions. You can look for the entities or data used in your system. The data will be the initial set of key abstractions. If you created a team collaboration diagram like Exhibit 6-6, you can use the business entities as your first set of key abstractions.

"First," Gus began, "let's look for things we store and retrieve."

"You mean the stuff we want in the database?" Dennis asked.

"Right."

"Okay, then, that's . . . order, product, and customer."

"Wait," Lisa added, "isn't customer part of order?"

"Maybe, but we won't know for sure until we try working with it. So we'll leave customer in for now."

"What about accounts?" asked Tara as she looked through the use cases.

"We never deal directly with accounts. The accounting system does, so we don't have to worry about them."

"Well, then, products are the same!"

"No, we actually do quite a bit with products."

"Sigh. All right, is that everything then?"

"No. What about the subsystems?"

"We can treat each subsystem as a system! Gus said so!" Tara said.

"She's right," Gus interjected.

"Well, then," Dennis said, "do the subsystems store and retrieve data?"

"They certainly use data."

"Anything we've missed so far?" Gus asked, looking up from his notes.

"Yes! Access permission! Or, rather, login information in general."

"Pick lists and mailing labels."

"Mailing label is just customer printed out. Good thing we made it a separate key abstraction."

"Let me catch up a second" Gus muttered as he wrote. "Okay, then. Let's fill these out with brief descriptions."

Key Abstractions for Order Processing

Order—at a minimum, a list of products with prices, shipping address, and payment information

Product—information about products, including at a minimum, product code, description, price, and stock on hand in the warehouse

Customer—information about a customer, including, at a minimum, name and address

User login info—at a minimum, username, password, and access restrictions

Pick list—list of products and quantities

Diagramming Scenarios with Key Abstractions

In Chapter 9 we created sequence diagrams for the use cases to test the subsystems and create interfaces. We can use the same technique with the key abstractions to verify that we have found all the key abstractions and to define their behavior.

Start with the simple sequence diagram you created in Chapter 5. Replace the system object with the key abstractions. Messages that went to the system object become messages to particular key abstractions. Alternatively, you can start with the subsystem level sequence diagram in Chapter 9 and replace subsystems with key abstractions. Messages to subsystems become messages to key abstractions. Key abstractions are represented by objects on the sequence diagram.

We start with the subsystem level sequence diagram (see Exhibit 11-1). We replace the subsystems with key abstractions and actors, and messages to subsystems with messages to key abstractions and actors. We also add messages to show the sequencing between the key abstractions (see Exhibit 11-2).

Exhibit 11-1 Place Order Subsystem Level Sequence Diagram

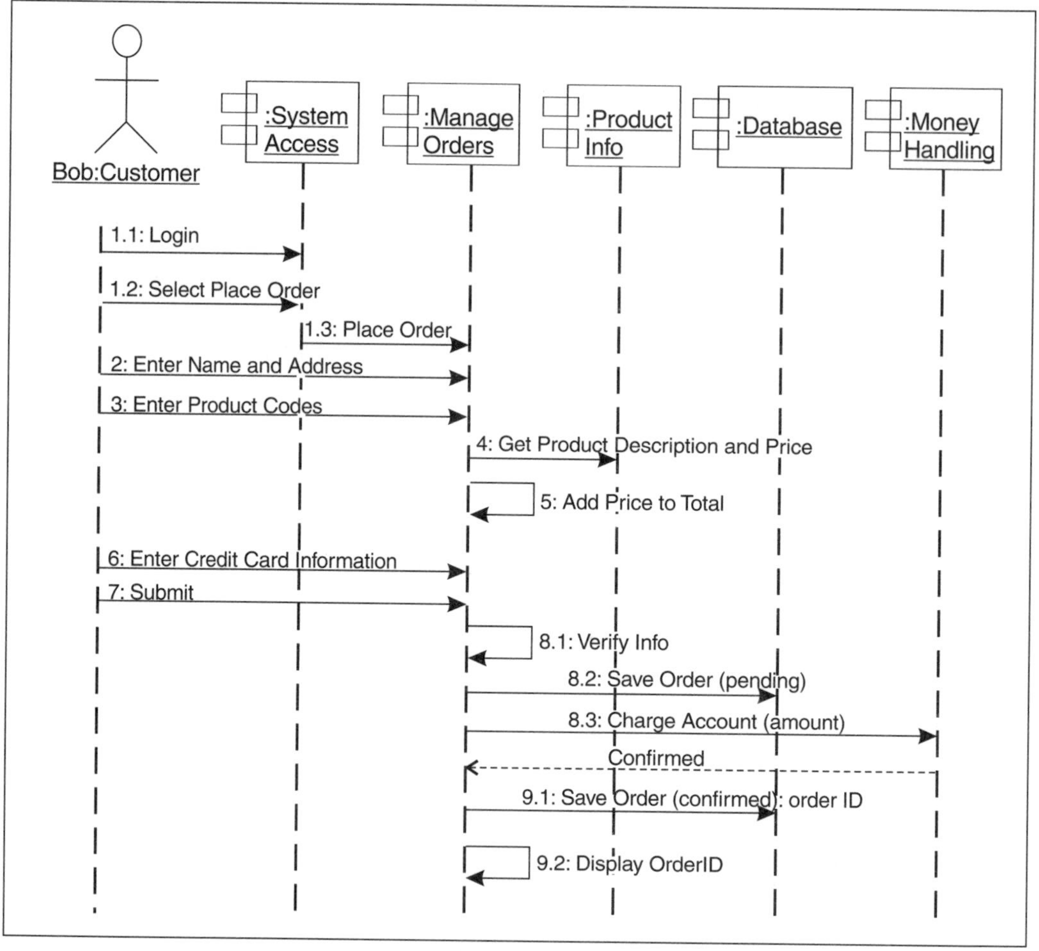

For example, the login message is handled by the Login Info key abstraction. We needed a way to display selections to the customer so that the customer can select Place Order. We added a User Selection object to do that work. We also added a display selections message from Login Info to User Selection. Another sequence starts with the message Select Place Order and leads to Create Order and Display Order. At that point the customer has a place to enter his name and address.

As you create the sequence diagrams, you may find that you need new things in your system. For example, during Place Order we needed something to allow the customer to choose Place Order. That didn't fit any of the original key abstractions, so we added a User Selection key abstraction to handle that behavior.

Exhibit 11-2   Place Order Key Abstraction Level Sequence Diagram

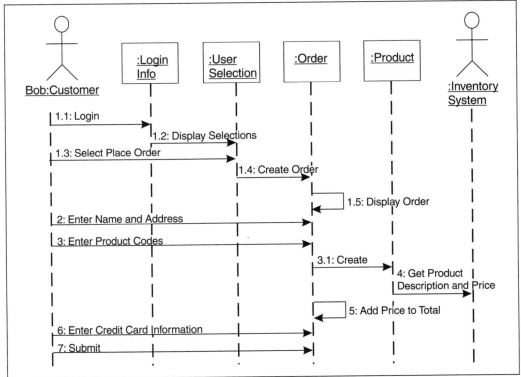

Diagramming Key Abstractions

The sequence diagrams helped us find which abstractions we needed to implement each use case. We also found messages that the abstractions had to respond to. We'll capture that information in a class diagram for each use case. We call this class diagram a view of participating classes for the use case. In the UML, we say this is a collaboration that realizes the use case.

We will use classes to represent the key abstractions. In the UML, a class is represented by a rectangle. Draw a rectangle for each key abstraction and divide it into three compartments. The first holds the name of the abstraction; the second describes the data it uses; and the third describes the messages it receives. For each use case, create a diagram showing the classes needed by that use case, as shown in Exhibit 11-3.

We got the information about the messages from the sequence diagram. We got the information about the data from the descriptions of the key abstractions. We don't show the customer or the inventory system because they are actors, not part of our system.

Exhibit 11-3 View of Participating Classes for the Place Order Use Case

LoginInfo	Order	User Selection
Username Password	OrderID CustomerInfo ListofProducts PaymentInfo	Selection
Login()		DisplaySelections() SelectPlaceOrder()
Product	CreateOrder() EnterNameAddress() EnterProductCodes() AddPriceToTotal() EnterCreditCard() Submit() DisplayOrder()	
ProductID Description Price		
Create()		

In the project plan, we identified use cases to develop for each iteration. The view of participating classes for those use cases tells us which classes to develop. The same class can appear on more than one view of participating classes. That simply means that part of the class will be used to implement one use case, and part of the class will be used to implement another use case.

In addition to creating class diagrams for use cases, we will also create one class diagram for each subsystem. This class diagram will contain the classes we need to implement the subsystem's behavior. In the UML, we say that this is a collaboration that realizes the subsystem. We can find the behavior by looking at the use case diagram for the subsystem, and by looking at the subsystem interface. A diagram for the manage orders subsystem is shown in Exhibit 11-4.

Classes inside a subsystem usually have much in common. Putting them together in a class diagram helps you find similarities between classes. Taking advantage of the similarities makes coding easier.

Use Case versus Subsystem View

We end up with two very different views of our system. The use case view shows the work flows throughout the system and helps us maintain consistency throughout that work flow. It is a good basis for black box testing and user guides because it shows the outside view of the system. The subsystem view shows the subsystems that make up the system and helps us maintain consistency within them. The subsystems are the basis of reuse and maintenance in your system. These are things you can buy if you decide not to build all of your system yourself.

Exhibit 11-4 Manage Orders Subsystem

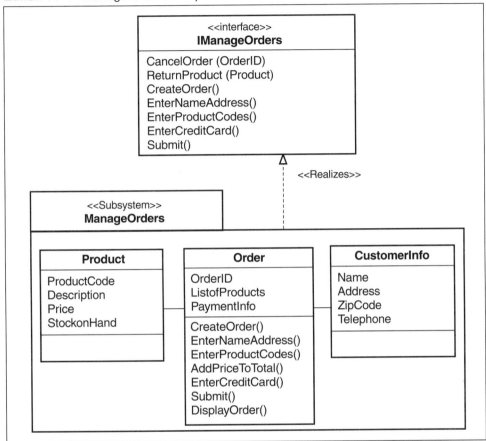

You may find it helpful to create a chart like the one in Exhibit 11-5, which shows how use cases relate to subsystems through classes. First, list use cases down one side; then list classes across the top using this naming convention:

```
subsystem::class name
```

Put an X in the box if the use case uses that class.

This chart helps make it clear that a use case describes a work flow through some of the classes in the architecture. Reading across the row, we see the classes that make up the use cases. Reading down the column, we see which use cases the class participates in.

This is a good time to combine all the classes for all the use cases onto one diagram. Review the diagram for consistency. You may decide to combine similar classes or rename classes for clarity. You may decide to split large

Exhibit 11-5 Classes and Scenarios

	SystemAccess::LoginInfo	SystemAccess::UserSelection	ManageOrders::Order	ManageOrders::Product	ProductInfo::InventorySystemInterface	ShipOrders::MailingLabel	ShipOrders::PickList
Place Order	X	X	X	X	X		

classes into several smaller classes. Use the same tests on classes that you used for testing subsystems in Chapter 9: functionality, coupling, cohesion, and communication.

THE ITERATION SCHEDULE

You are ready to start the first iteration. Looking at the project plan, you know how long you have to build it, what you are going to build, and how you are going to test it. Spend a little time at the beginning of the iteration reviewing this information with your team. Determine dependencies in the software and make sure that the software used by most of the team is developed first.

Set aside some time at the end of the iteration to review it, update documentation, and firm up plans for the next two iterations. Imagine that the first iteration is scheduled for September 1 through September 22.

- Sept. 1 — plan the work assignments.
- Sept. 2 through Sept. 21 — code the first set of use cases
  - Login, basic path only
- Sept. 22 — review and plan the next set of activities.

The coding part of the iteration includes analysis, design, coding, and testing. See Appendix A for books about software development and testing.

Because use cases describe the behavior of the system, we can use them to test the code. Does the software act and react as described in the use cases? If not, why?

At the end of the iteration, take some time to review and update all project documentation.

- Look at what you actually accomplished and compare it to the goals for this iteration. Did you meet your goals? Why or why not? If some use cases did not get built, where will they go in the project plan?
- What did you learn about risk factors? Do changes need to be made to your list of risks? If so, how does that affect your project plan?
- Look at your use cases. Did any change? Did any go away? Did you add new use cases? Where do they fit in your project plan?
- Look at the actors. Did any change or go away? Did you add new actors? What happens to the use cases associated with these actors?
- What changes did you make to your architecture?

Go back and update your project documents to reflect any changes you need to make because of what you learned. Update your project plan as needed, focusing especially on the next two iterations.

You also may need to schedule a project review with management, marketing, sales, or end users. Use your updated project documents to pull together a presentation. Is there something you can demo in your current system? You might be able to demo by creating a quick command line interface to your code if the user interface does not yet exist.

DELIVERY AND BEYOND

This phase of project development is where you turn your system into a product. Some of the things created in this transition phase are:

- User guides
- Training materials
- Sales kits
- Demos
- Marketing plans
- Ad campaigns

The documentation you have been creating, particularly use cases, will help you develop these documents.

As the project progresses, you must keep the documents up to date. Many people are depending on the information to be correct. The ultimate success of the project depends on all parts working together—the system with its validated testing, user manuals, training, and sales kits.

You won't want to share all of the documentation but only the parts that represent what you are actually delivering. You may have use cases for everything you will eventually do with a product, but the first version being delivered to customers may implement only a subset of them. The rest will come in a later release. You won't want user guides or training covering features that don't exist yet. You also don't want sales or marketing to tell customers about features that the product won't have.

User Guides and Training

Technical writers will want the descriptions of use cases and their scenarios as the basis for user guides. Each use case, with its alternatives and exceptions, describes to users how the system behaves and how they interact with it. The use cases can be put together with screen shots of the user interface as a starting point for a user guide.

This first cut at a user guide can also be a starting point for training materials for end users. You will want to put the material in a slide format and create exercises, but the basic information you need to use the system is in the use cases.

Sales Kits and Marketing Literature

Use cases can be the basis for the "What our product does" part of sales kits and marketing material. Looking through the use cases, marketing people can find the features you are building. Be sure marketing knows what you are actually delivering. The use cases you share may be only a subset of all of the possible use cases.

The project plan will also be of interest to marketing. With information on what features will be finished when, they can design alpha and beta release programs, and develop product announcements and plan advertising campaigns.

Marketing or the engineering team may want to put together demos of the product. The steps of the use cases can be put together to create a script showing the functionality of the system.

Use Cases After Delivery

The use cases you have written contain much information about your domain as well as about the system you have actually built. This information is historical but can also be used as a basis for a repository of information for developing a line of business.

The next project you construct in the same domain will have many similarities to the current project. The new team can look over the existing use cases and modify them for the new system. This is a lot faster than redeveloping all this information each time a project is started.

The use cases are also a repository of knowledge that can be shared with new employees. In most cases, when someone is hired for a project, he or she obtains information about it from the other people working on it. Having a set of use cases to review gives the new person a lot of information without taking time from other team members. This knowledge store also is available when key people leave the project or the company. The people are no longer available, but what they knew about the project is captured in the use cases and their associated information.

CHAPTER REVIEW

In this chapter, we looked at numerous possible uses of use cases in construction, delivery, and beyond. There are many good books on software development and software testing. For more information on these topics, interested readers should refer to Appendix A.

Things you may have created during this phase of development include those shown in Table 11-1.

Table 11-1 Construction Phase Deliverables

Complete	Deliverables
✔	Iteration plans
✔	Code
✔	Test plans
✔	Test results
✔	Review of iteration
✔	User guides
✔	Training manuals
✔	Demos
✔	Sales and marketing materials

FINAL WRAP-UP

We can't promise that if you follow the steps your software will be wonderful. We do believe that you will understand your project better, which is the first step toward building better systems. You will spend a lot of time on analysis — probably 25 percent of the total project schedule. But this time is made up later during construction because the project's problems were addressed at the beginning. Working with use cases tends to bring out project issues early. It's better to deal with them in analysis than when everyone is busy coding.

Like any project, this book had deadlines to meet. Although we would like to say that it is perfect in every way, we must admit that we are continuing to work on the material. The UML is currently going through a review process, and we expect some of that work to affect future editions. Where can you get the most up-to-date information? Visit our Web site at *http://books.txt.com* or e-mail us at *books@txt.com*.

Appendix A

Resources

This appendix includes a short list of books we have found interesting and thought-provoking over the years. We've included books about OOAD, project management, patterns and idioms, architecture, sociology, and market trends. We like to look at software projects from a variety of perspectives, so some of these books are not about software, specifically; still, they have stimulated thought and given us new perspectives on software development.

Bellin, D., Simone, S. 1997. *The CRC Card Book*. Reading, MA: Addison-Wesley.

CRC cards are a great team approach to determining the responsibilities of classes and their collaborations with other classes. They are especially nice for groups new to OO.

Booch, G. 1996. *Best of Booch*. New York: SIGS Books.

A collection of essays on everything to do with software development.

Booch, G. 1994. *Object-Oriented Analysis and Design with Application, Second Edition*. Reading, MA: Addison-Wesley.

A good book on object-oriented analysis and design.

Booch, G. 1996. *Object Solutions*. Reading, MA: Addison-Wesley.

A great explanation of managing your software project.

Brand, S. 1994. *How Buildings Learn*. New York: Penguin Books.

An interesting book on the architecture of buildings, but Chapter 11, "The Scenario-Buffered Building", contains good information that can apply to software.

Brooks, F. 1995. *The Mythical Man-Month: Anniversary Edition*. Reading, MA: Addison-Wesley.

A classic must-read.

Buschmann, F., R. Meunier, H. Rohnert, P. Sommerlad, and M. Stal. 1996. *Pattern-Oriented Software Architecture: A System of Patterns.* West Sussex, England: Wiley.

> A good book on software architecture patterns and design patterns extending the work of Gamma et al.

Fowler, M. 1997. *Analysis Patterns.* Reading, MA: Addison-Wesley.

> Patterns applied to problems at the analysis stage of software development.

Fowler, M. with K. Scott. 2000. *UML Distilled: Applying the Standard Object Modeling Language, Second Edition.* Menlo Park, CA: Addison-Wesley.

> With all the UML books out, this is still the best overview of the core parts of the UML—the parts everyone can use.

Gamma, E., R. Helm, R. Johnson, and J. Vlissides. 1995. *Design Patterns: Elements of Object-Oriented Architecture.* Reading, MA: Addison-Wesley.

> The book on design patterns. Describes well-known design problems and gives patterns of solutions. Everyone refers to this as the "GOF" (Gang of Four) book.

Hohmann, L. 1997. *Journey of the Software Professional: A Sociology of Software Development.* Upper Saddle River, NJ: Prentice-Hall.

> The care and feeding of your development team. A must-read for managers, with many great parts for programmers as well. How do engineers think? How do we create teams that can work together? What kind of environment do engineers need to be most effective on the job?

Jacobson, I., M. Christerson, P. Jonsson, and G. Oevergaard. 1992. *Object-Oriented Software Engineering.* New York: ACM Press.

> The original use case book. Jacobson's methodology has been largely incorporated into the UML. This is an alternate view of software development from Booch and Rumbaugh. Combined in the UML, these methodologies help you develop a more well-rounded application.

Jacobson, I., M. Ericsson, and A. Jacobson. 1995. *The Object Advantage.* Reading, MA: Addison-Wesley.

> Applies OO techniques and use cases to business processes.

Popcorn, F., and L. Marigold. 1996. *Clicking.* New York: HarperCollins.

Popcorn, F. 1992. *The Popcorn Report.* New York: HarperCollins.

> These two books are on market trends in society. These might be useful for ideas when doing risk analysis for your product.

Rumbaugh, J., M. Blaha, W. Premerlani, F. Eddy, and W. Lorensen. 1991. *Object-Oriented Modeling and Design.* Englewood Cliffs, NJ: Prentice-Hall.

> Another classic OOAD book. The notation is quite similar to UML.

Rumbaugh, J. 1996. *OMT Insights.* New York: SIGS Books.

> A collection of articles on software development.

Shaw, M. and D. Garlan. 1996. *Software Architecture: Perspectives on an Emerging Discipline.* Englewood Cliffs, NJ: Prentice-Hall.

> A well-written book on software architecture patterns. Great for ideas when developing your own architectures.

Taylor, D. 1998. *Object-Oriented Technology: A Manager's Guide, Second Edition.* Reading, MA: Addison-Wesley.

> Need an easy book on OO terminology for managers? This is it. No one has done it better.

Webster, B. 1995. *Pitfalls of Object Oriented Development.* New York: M & T Books.

> We all know that sometimes things go a bit wrong on a project. This book lists a number of pitfalls, tells how you to detect when you are in trouble, and what to do to correct the situation.

Here are a couple of our favorite books for those times when you need to rest the conscious brain and let the subconscious work on the problem.

Anthony, Piers. Any of the *Xanth* books—there are about 20 of them. Published by Del Ray, Avon, and Tor.

> Definitely light reading, but if you like puns, you'll love these books.

Eddings, David. *The Belgariad and the Mallorean* series. About 12 rather thick books. Published by Del Ray.

> Good guys, bad guys, and fair maidens to be won. But the characters are deep, fully formed, and interesting.

McKinley, Robin. 1978. *Beauty.* New York: Pocket Books.

> The best telling of the Beauty and the Beast story, ever. You might cry. It's okay.

Appendix B

Documentation Templates

These templates have been written up for Adobe FrameMaker, Microsoft Word, and as text files. They can be found at *http://books.txt.com*

SYSTEM OR SUBSYSTEM DOCUMENTS

System Name
<Brief description. In a large system, this can be several pages. Note that this is not meant to be detailed requirements, but to be a basic overview of the system.>

Risk Factors
<List risk factors for the project in priority order.>

System-Level Use Case Diagram
<One or more use case diagrams showing all the use cases and actors in the system. This does not have to include relationships between use cases such as include, extend, or generalization.>

Architecture Diagram
<Include a description of the interfaces as well. These can be in the diagram or listed in text.>

Subsystem Descriptions
<Include a brief description of each subsystem.>

USE CASE DOCUMENTS

Use Case Name

Brief Description
<Usually a paragraph or less. May include the priority and status of this use case.>

Context Diagram
<A small use case diagram showing this use case and all its relationships.>

Preconditions
<A list of conditions that must be true before the use case starts.>

Flow of Events
<A section for the basic path and each alternative path.>

Postconditions
<A list of conditions that must be true when the use case ends, no matter which path is executed.>

Subordinate Use Cases Diagram
<A small use case diagram showing the subordinate use cases of this use case.>

Subordinate Use Cases
<A section for each subordinate use case with its flow of events.>

Activity Diagram
<A diagram of the flow of events or some significant or complex part of the flow of events.>

View of Participating Classes
<A class diagram showing the classes that collaborate to implement this use case.>

Sequence Diagrams
<One or more sequence diagrams for the basic path and alternatives.>

User Interface
<Sketches or screen shots showing the user interface. Possibly storyboards.>

Business Rules

<A list of the business rules implemented by this use case.>

Special Requirements

<A list of the special requirements that pertain to this use case—for example, timing, sizing, or usability.>

Other Artifacts

<This can include references to the subsystem the use case belongs to, an analysis model, a design model, code, or test plans.>

Outstanding Issues

<A list of questions pertaining to this use case that need to be answered.>

UML Notation

This appendix contains only a subset of the UML notation used in this book. It is not intended to teach the notation but to provide a quick reference to the revelant parts.

Use Case Diagram Notation

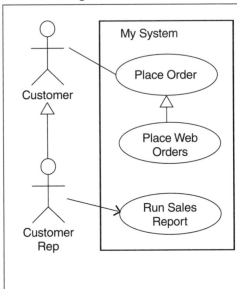

Actors are Customer and Customer Rep. Use cases are Place Order, Run Sales Report, and Place Web Orders.

Customer Rep inherits from Customer, so Customer Rep may use Place Order as well as Run Sales Report. Customer may use only Place Order. Place Web Orders inherits behavior from Place Order and adds more behavior.

The communicates relationship is between actor and use case. The arrow shows who starts the use case. Customer Rep starts Run Sales Report. We don't know who starts Place Order.

The rectangle around the use cases marks the system boundary. The name of the system or subsystem is inside the rectangle.

Use Case Diagram Notation (*Continued*)

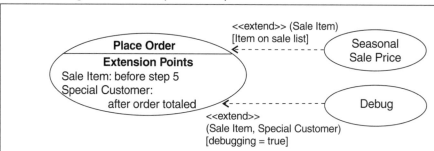

Place Order use case with extension points. Seasonal Sale Price and Debug are both extending Place Order.

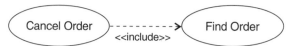

Cancel Order use case includes the Find Order use case.

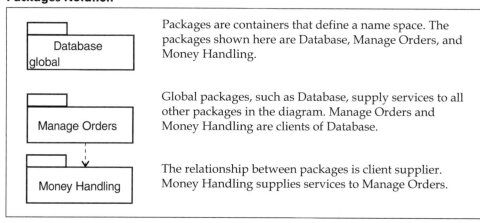

Inventory System has an interface called IUpdateProducts. Place Order communicates with Inventory System by using its interface. Place Order has an interface called IPlaceOrder. Big Batch System communicates with Place Order by using its interface.

Packages Notation

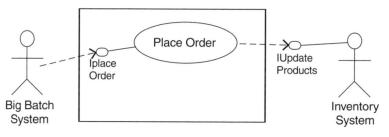

Packages are containers that define a name space. The packages shown here are Database, Manage Orders, and Money Handling.

Global packages, such as Database, supply services to all other packages in the diagram. Manage Orders and Money Handling are clients of Database.

The relationship between packages is client supplier. Money Handling supplies services to Manage Orders.

Activity Diagram Notation

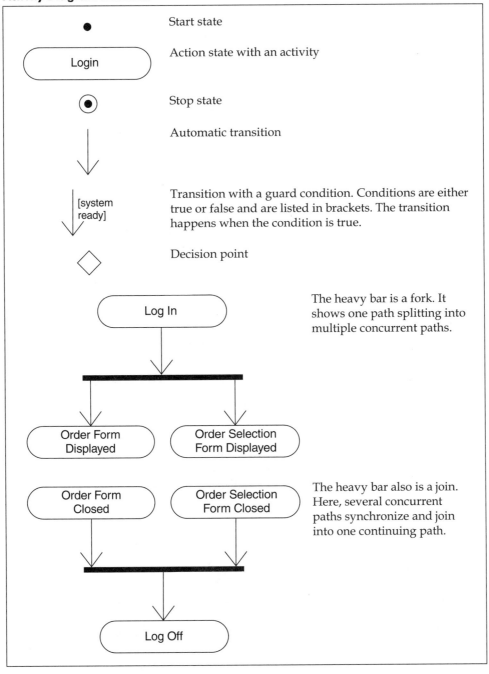

Start state

Action state with an activity

Stop state

Automatic transition

Transition with a guard condition. Conditions are either true or false and are listed in brackets. The transition happens when the condition is true.

Decision point

The heavy bar is a fork. It shows one path splitting into multiple concurrent paths.

The heavy bar also is a join. Here, several concurrent paths synchronize and join into one continuing path.

Sequence Diagram Notation

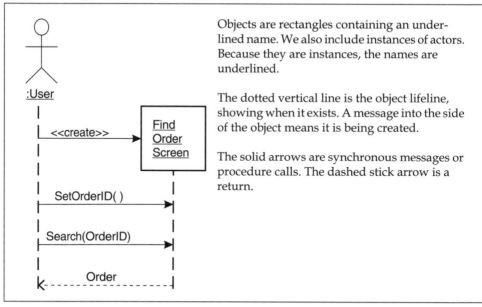

Objects are rectangles containing an under-lined name. We also include instances of actors. Because they are instances, the names are underlined.

The dotted vertical line is the object lifeline, showing when it exists. A message into the side of the object means it is being created.

The solid arrows are synchronous messages or procedure calls. The dashed stick arrow is a return.

Class Diagram Notation

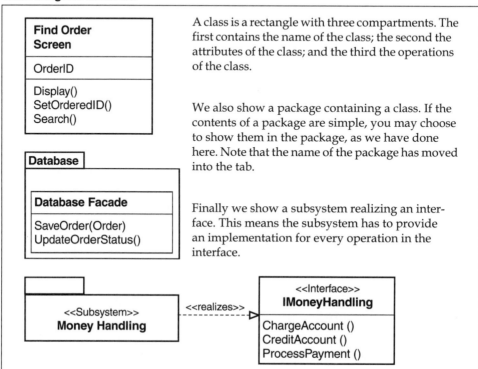

A class is a rectangle with three compartments. The first contains the name of the class; the second the attributes of the class; and the third the operations of the class.

We also show a package containing a class. If the contents of a package are simple, you may choose to show them in the package, as we have done here. Note that the name of the package has moved into the tab.

Finally we show a subsystem realizing an inter-face. This means the subsystem has to provide an implementation for every operation in the interface.

Business Process Notation

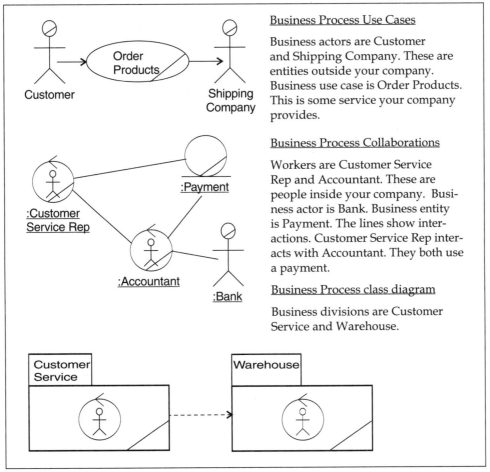

Business Process Use Cases

Business actors are Customer and Shipping Company. These are entities outside your company. Business use case is Order Products. This is some service your company provides.

Business Process Collaborations

Workers are Customer Service Rep and Accountant. These are people inside your company. Business actor is Bank. Business entity is Payment. The lines show interactions. Customer Service Rep interacts with Accountant. They both use a payment.

Business Process class diagram

Business divisions are Customer Service and Warehouse.

Appendix D

Sending Results of the Use Case Estimator

We are interested in continuing the work on estimating projects with use cases. If you try the use case estimator, we would be interested in hearing from you. Did it give you accurate results? Would you modify it? How and why?

In addition we would like a brief description of your project—for example, something like: It was a small distributed business application, with a project team of five people, two of whom were expert in object orientation with the rest new to it. The code was written in Visual Basic and used CORBA, which the whole team knew quite well.

If you are able to include your project description, we would be interested in seeing that as well. Did you change any of the weights? Which ones and why?

Did you find the factors useful? Did you add or delete any factors? Which ones and why?

You can send us the information via e-mail at *books@txt.com*

For the curious, we did get a number of e-mails after the first edition, all of which asked if anyone else had tried this estimator. We have used it some, and think that in general it produces optimistic estimates. The estimator probably gives the best results when your team is experienced and everyone is full-time on the project.

For your information, we have reproduced the technical and environmental factors tables here.

Technical Factors for System and Weights

Factor Number	Factor Description	Weight
T1	Distributed system	2
T2	Response or throughput performance objectives	1
T3	End user efficiency (on line)	1
T4	Complex internal processing	1
T5	Code must be reusable	1
T6	Easy to install	0.5
T7	Easy to use	0.5
T8	Portable	2
T9	Easy to change	1
T10	Concurrent	1
T11	Includes special security features	1
T12	Provides direct access for third parties	1
T13	Special user training facilities required	1

Environmental Factors for Team and Weights

Factor Number	Factor Description	Weight
F1	Familiar with Rational Unified Process	1.5
F2	Application experience	0.5
F3	Object-oriented experience	1
F4	Lead analyst capability	0.5
F5	Motivation	1
F6	Stable requirements	2
F7	Part-time workers	–1
F8	Difficult programming language	–1

Appendix E

Order-Processing System

In real life, the use cases for a small system will be fairly well worked out before work begins on building the system. Large systems tend to work more in parallel than linearly. This means that some people will work on use cases while others will start building code for the use cases already completed. Because our order-processing system is relatively small, we completed all the use cases for it before building the system. We did not detail the alternatives, however, because they seemed pretty simple. If we find out later that they are relatively complex, we can write out detailed descriptions.

This appendix contains a set of documentation for the Order-Processing System described throughout the book. Don't feel that you have to read all of it. Just browse a bit to get a feel for the documentation. Here are a few things to look for.

You'll see a lot of include relationships between use cases, but no extend. *Include* relationships are found early in the process and allow you to show commonality between parts of the system. *Extend* relationships tend to be added later, when you find some new requirement or functionality that extends the current system. Since we haven't built the first system yet, we don't have anything to extend.

We're not entirely happy with the process for handling back-ordered items, but since it seems to work, we'll go with it for now. This is an area we'll revisit later to make the process more efficient. Right now our focus is on getting a working system completed.

Look at what happened to some of the include relationships. A use case must be completely contained within a system or subsystem, except for communicates relationships with actors. This means that we cannot have an include relationship from a use case in one subsystem to a use case in another subsystem. The Place Order use case in the system-level use case diagram includes the Get Product Information use case. But these use cases ended up in different subsystems—Place Order in the Manage Orders subsystem and Get Product Information in the Product Information subsystem. Our include relationship at the system level becomes a communicates relationship in the subsystems. You will see this in a number of places in the following pages.

ORDER-PROCESSING SYSTEM

We are developing order-processing software for a mail order company called National Widgets, which is a reseller of products purchased from various suppliers. Twice a year the company publishes a catalog of products, which is mailed to customers and other interested people.

Customers purchase products by submitting a list of products with payment to National Widgets. National Widgets fills the order and ships the products to the customer's address. The order-processing software will track the order from the time it is received until the product is shipped.

National Widgets provides quick service. They should be able to ship a customer's order by the fastest, most efficient means possible. Customers may return items for restocking, but sometimes will pay a fee.

Risk Factors

- Will the inexperience of some of the software designers create problems?
- How can we prevent lost orders on system failure?
- How can we make the system easy for nontechnical people to use?
- Can we be successful if we don't support a Web interface?
- What if the system is immediately flooded with orders?
- How do we handle many simultaneous users in different parts of the company?
- How do we handle the database crashing?

SYSTEM-LEVEL USE CASES

Order-Processing Use Case

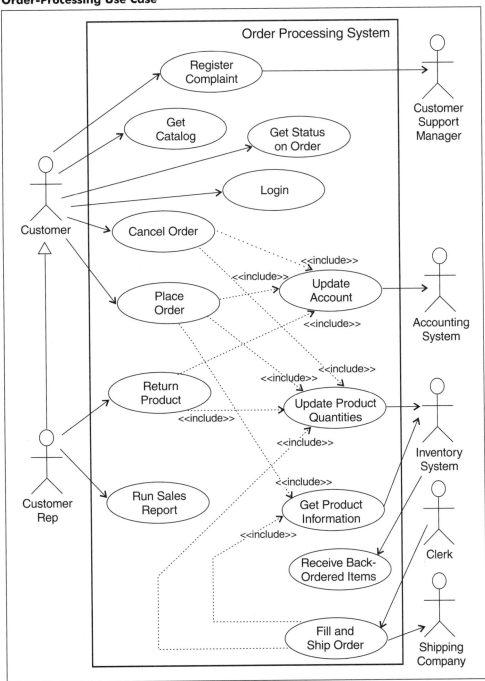

ARCHITECTURE

Order-Processing Architecture

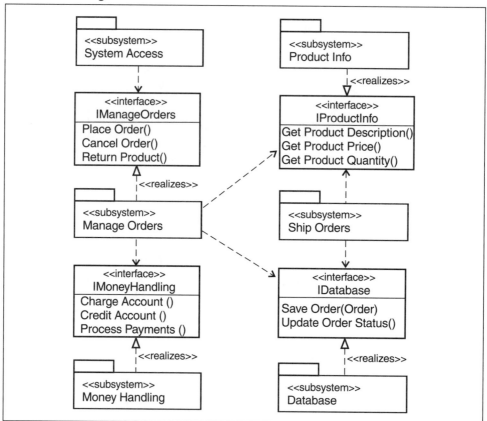

System Access Subsystem

This subsystem handles login and logout, and checks for access permissions.

Product Information Subsystem

This subsystem provides all kinds of information about products. It interfaces with the inventory system.

Manage Orders Subsystem

This subsystem handles order taking, product returns, order status, and order cancellation.

Ship Orders Subsystem

This subsystem prints pick lists for orders, generates mailing labels, and calculates shipping and handling for orders.

Money Handling Subsystem

This subsystem interfaces with the accounting system, updates accounts, charges and credits customers, and handles checks, credit cards, and money orders.

Database Subsystem

This subsystem contains the data we have to store for the application. It provides standard store, retrieve, update, and delete functions for the data that is stored.

LOGIN

Brief Description

This use case describes the process by which users log in to the order-processing system. It also sets up access permissions for various categories of users.

Context Diagram

Login Context Diagram

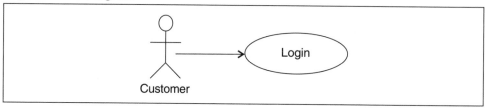

Preconditions

Flow of Events

Basic Path

1. The use case begins when the user starts the application.
2. The system displays the Login screen.
3. The user enters a username and password.
4. The system verifies the information.
5. The system sets access permissions.
6. The system displays the Main screen (subordinate use case: Display Main Screen)
7. The use case ends.

Alternative Paths

- Bad username.
- Bad password.
- User does not have a username and password for our system.
- User selects a function for which she is not allowed access.
- User makes no selection of function.

Postconditions

Subordinate Use Cases Diagram

Login Subordinate Use Cases Diagram

Subordinate Use Cases

Get User Record

Basic Path

1. The use case begins when a request is received to get a user record.
2. The system locates the user record using the username.
3. The system returns the user record to the requestor.
4. The use case ends.

Display Main Screen

Basic Path

1. The use case begins when a request is received to display the Main screen.
2. The system determines which functions are allowed for this user, based on access rights set during login.
3. The system displays the Main screen with the appropriate functions available for selection by the user.
4. The use case ends.

Activity Diagram

Login Primary Scenario

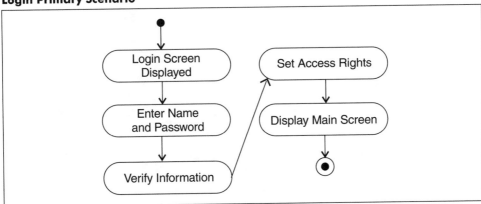

View of Participating Classes

Sequence Diagrams

User Interface

Login Screen

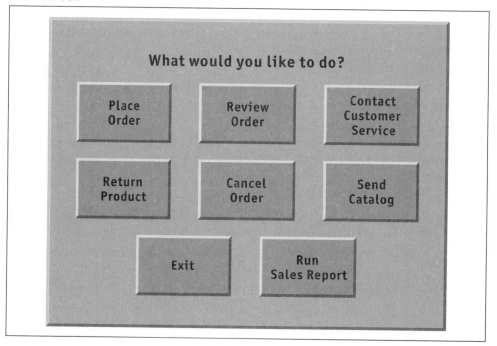

Main Screen

Business Rules

Special Requirements

Other Artifacts

Outstanding Issues

PLACE ORDER

Brief Description

This use case describes the process by which orders are entered into the order-processing system.

Context Diagram

Place Order Context Diagram

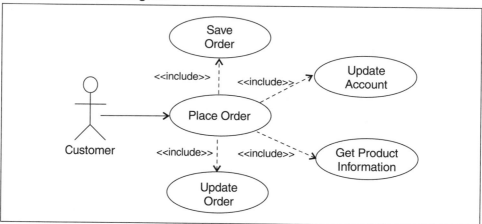

Preconditions

Flow of Events

Basic Path

1. The use case begins when the customer selects Place Order.
2. The system displays the Place Order screen.
3. The customer enters his or her name and address.
4. The customer enters product codes for products to be ordered.
5. For each product code entered
   a) Include Get Product Information
   b) The system adds the price of the item to the total.
end loop
6. The customer enters credit card payment information.
7. The customer selects Submit.
8. The system verifies the information.
9. The system saves the order as pending — Include Save Order.

10. Include Update Account.
11. The system marks the order confirmed.
12. Include Update Order.
13. The system returns an order ID to the customer, and the use case ends.

Alternative Paths

- Payment not there.
- Shipping address incomplete.
- Product code doesn't match actual products.
- Product no longer carried.
- Payment bad.
- Customer pays by check.
- Customer sends order by mail.
- Customer phones in order.

Alternative Path: Cancel Placing an Order

Precondition: The user did not select Submit.

1. The alternative begins when the user selects Cancel.
2. The system discards any entered information.
3. The system returns to the previous display.
4. The use case ends.

Postconditions

Subordinate Use Cases Diagram

Subordinate Use Cases

Activity Diagram

Place Order Primary Scenario

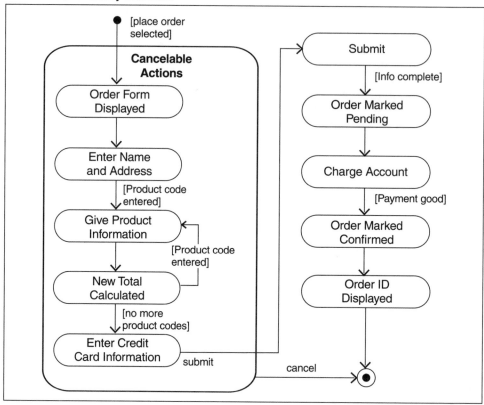

View of Participating Classes

Sequence Diagrams

User Interface

Place Order Screen

Shipping Name	
Shipping Address	
City, State, ZIP	

Product Code	Description	Quantity	Price Each	Total Price

Subtotal
Tax
Total

| Credit Card Number | |
| Expiration Date | |

Order ID

[Cancel] [Submit]

Business Rules

Special Requirements

Other Artifacts

Outstanding Issues

SAVE ORDER

Brief Description

This use case describes the process by which orders are entered into the order-processing system.

Context Diagram

Save Order Context Diagram

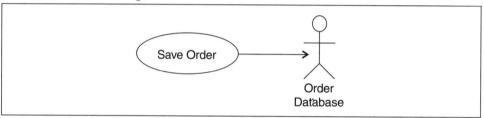

Preconditions

Flow of Events

Basic Path

1. The use case begins when a request is received to save a new order.
2. The system sets the order status to pending.
3. The system requests that the order database store the order.
4. The order database returns a unique order ID.
5. The system returns the order ID to the requestor.
6. The use case ends.

Alternative Paths

- Database not available.

Postconditions

Subordinate Use Cases Diagram

Subordinate Use Cases

Activity Diagram

View of Participating Classes

Sequence Diagrams

User Interface

Business Rules

Special Requirements

Other Artifacts

Outstanding Issues

UPDATE ORDER

Brief Description

This use case describes how orders are updated in the order database.

Context Diagram

Update Order Context Diagram

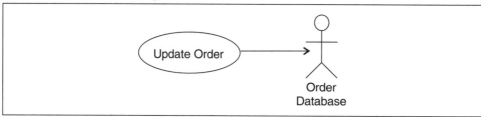

Preconditions

Flow of Events

Basic Path

1. The use case begins when a request is received to update an existing order.
2. The system sends the changed fields to the database with the order ID and a request to update the order records.
3. The database returns a confirmation.
4. The use case ends.

Alternative Paths

- Database not available.

Postconditions

Subordinate Use Cases Diagram

Subordinate Use Cases

Activity Diagram

View of Participating Classes

Sequence Diagrams

User Interface

Business Rules

Special Requirements

Other Artifacts

Outstanding Issues

GET PRODUCT INFORMATION

Brief Description

This use case retrieves product information from the inventory system.

Context Diagram

Get Product Information Context Diagram

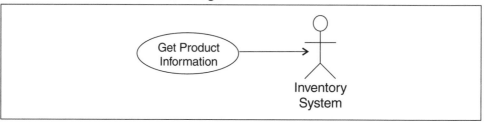

Preconditions

Flow of Events

Basic Path

1. The use case begins when a product code is entered.
2. The system sends a request to the inventory system for product information based on that product code.
3. The inventory system returns the product information, which must include at least product description, price, and stock on hand.
4. The use case ends.

Alternative Paths

- No such product.
- Product no longer carried.
- Inventory system unavailable.

Postconditions

Subordinate Use Cases Diagram

Subordinate Use Cases

Activity Diagram

View of Participating Classes

Sequence Diagrams

User Interface

Business Rules

Special Requirements

Other Artifacts

Outstanding Issues

UPDATE ACCOUNT

Brief Description

This use case interacts with the accounting system to apply charges or credits to an account.

Context Diagram

Update Account Context Diagram

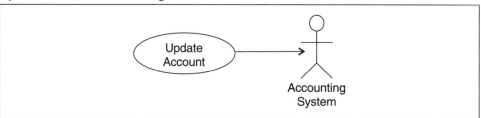

Preconditions

Flow of Events

Basic Path

1. The use case begins when a request to update an account is received.
2. The system sends credit card information and the amount of credit or debit to the accounting system.
3. The accounting system sends a status of Okay.
4. The use case ends.

Alternative Paths

- Account overdrawn.
- Account doesn't exist.
- Accounting system not available.

Postconditions

Subordinate Use Cases Diagram

Subordinate Use Cases

Activity Diagram

View of Participating Classes

Sequence Diagrams

User Interface

Business Rules

Special Requirements

Other Artifacts

Outstanding Issues

RETURN PRODUCT

Brief Description

This use case describes the process by which unwanted products are returned to the company by the customer.

Context Diagram

Return Product Context Diagram

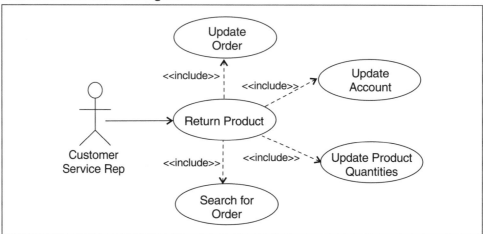

Preconditions

Flow of Events

Basic Path

1. The use case begins when the customer rep selects Return Product.
2. Include Search for Order.
3. The system displays the selected order in the Return Products screen.
4. The customer rep selects the products to return.
5. The customer rep selects Submit.
6. Include Update Account.
7. Include Update Product Quantities.
8. Include Update Order
9. The system displays an acknowledgment and the use case ends.

Alternative Paths

• No orders for this customer.
• Order ID not found in system.

- Customer not found in system.
- Account no longer valid.
- Accounting system not available.
- Inventory system not available.

Postconditions

Subordinate Use Cases Diagram

Subordinate Use Cases

Activity Diagram

View of Participating Classes

Sequence Diagrams

User Interface

Return Product Screen

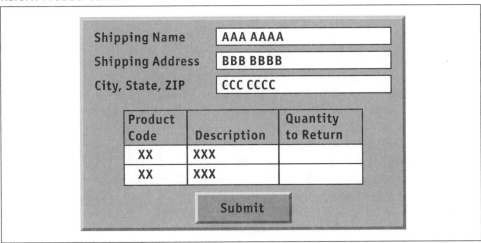

Business Rules

Special Requirements

Other Artifacts

Outstanding Issues

SEARCH FOR ORDER

Brief Description

This use case describes the process for finding a particular order in the system.

Context Diagram

Search for Order Context Diagram

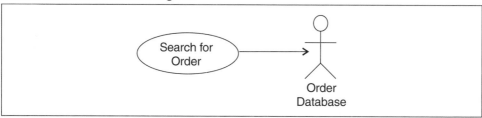

Preconditions

Flow of Events

Basic Path

1. The use case begins when the Find Order screen is displayed.
2. The user enters an order ID or name and address.
3. The user selects Search.
4. The system queries the database to get the orders requested.
5. If the user entered a name and address
   a) The system displays a list of orders for that customer, including at least order ID and date of order.
   b) The user selects one order.
   end if
6. The system returns the selected order and the use case ends.

Alternative Paths

- No orders for this customer.
- Order ID not found in system.
- No such customer.
- Database not available.

Postconditions

Subordinate Use Cases Diagram

Subordinate Use Cases Diagram

Subordinate Use Cases

Get Order List

Basic Path

1. The use case begins when a request for an order list is received.
2. The system sends the name and address to the order database with a query for all orders for this customer.
3. The database returns a list of all records found that match the name and address submitted. The list must include at least an order ID and the date the order was placed for each order in the list.
4. The use case ends.

Get Order

Basic Path

1. The use case begins when a request for an order is received.
2. The system sends the order ID to the order database with a query for the order matching this identifier.
3. The database returns zero or one order matching the identifier.
4. The use case ends.

Activity Diagram

View of Participating Classes

Sequence Diagrams

User Interface

Find Order Screen

Order Selection Screen

Business Rules

Special Requirements

Other Artifacts

Outstanding Issues

UPDATE PRODUCT QUANTITIES

Brief Description

This use case interfaces with the inventory system to update product quantities in the inventory.

Context Diagram

Update Product Quantities Context Diagram

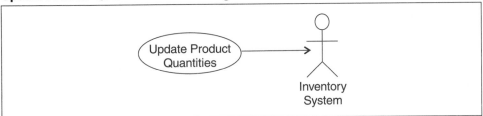

Preconditions

Flow of Events

Basic Path

1. The use case begins when a request to update product quantities is received.
2. If the quantity is positive then
    The system will send a request to the inventory system to add that amount to the stock on hand for a product.
3. Otherwise, if the quantity is not positive, the system sends a request to the inventory system to subtract that amount from the stock on hand for a product.
end if
4. The inventory system sends an acknowledgment, and the use case ends.

Alternative Paths

- Inventory system not available.
- Product no longer stocked.

Postconditions

Subordinate Use Cases Diagram

Subordinate Use Cases

Activity Diagram

View of Participating Classes

Sequence Diagrams

User Interface

Business Rules

Special Requirements

Other Artifacts

Outstanding Issues

CANCEL ORDER

Brief Description

This use case describes the process by which a customer can cancel an order.

Context Diagram

Cancel Order Context Diagram

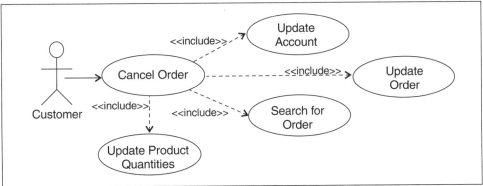

Preconditions

Flow of Events

Basic Path

1. The use case starts when the customer selects Cancel Order.
2. The customer selects an order to cancel—Include Search for Order.
3. The system displays the Cancel Order screen for that order.
4. The customer selects Cancel.
5. If the order has not been shipped
   a) The system deletes the order from the database—Include Update Order.
   b) The system credits the customer—Include Update Account.
   c) The system releases items in the order back to inventory—Include Update Product Quantities.
6. Otherwise, display Return Policies screen.
end if
7. The use case ends.

Alternative Paths

- No orders for this customer.
- Order ID not found in system.

- Customer not found in system.
- Account no longer valid.
- Accounting system not available.

Postconditions

Subordinate Use Cases Diagram

Subordinate Use Cases

Activity Diagram

View of Participating Classes

Sequence Diagrams

User Interface

Return Policies Screen

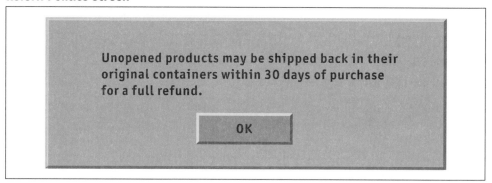

Unopened products may be shipped back in their original containers within 30 days of purchase for a full refund.

OK

Cancel Order Screen

Shipping Name	
Shipping Address	
City, State, ZIP	

Product Code	Description	Quantity	Price Each	Total Price

Subtotal

Tax

Total

Are you sure you want to cancel this order?

| Cancel Order | Keep Order |

Business Rules

Special Requirements

Other Artifacts

Outstanding Issues

GET STATUS ON ORDER

Brief Description

This use case describes the process by which customers can get the current status on any of their orders.

Context Diagram

Get Status on Order Context Diagram

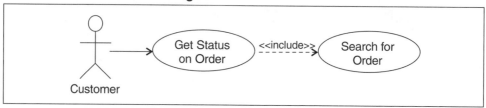

Preconditions

Flow of Events

Basic Path

1. The use case starts when the user selects Review Order.
2. Include Search for Order.
3. The system displays the Get Status on Order screen, and the use case ends.

Alternative Paths

• Order not found.

Postconditions

Subordinate Use Cases Diagram

Subordinate Use Cases

Activity Diagram

View of Participating Classes

Sequence Diagrams

User Interface

Get Status on Order Screen

Shipping Name			
Order ID	Status		OK

Product	Description	Quantity	Item Status

Business Rules

Special Requirements

Other Artifacts

GET CATALOG

Brief Description

This use case describes how a customer can request a catalog.

Context Diagram

Get Catalog Context Diagram

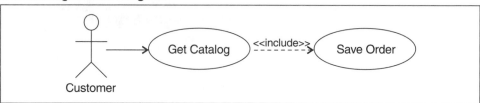

Preconditions

Flow of Events

Basic Path

1. The use case starts when the customer selects Get Catalog.
2. The Order Catalog screen is displayed.
3. The user enters a name and address.
4. The user selects Submit.
5. The system creates an order for a catalog product and a total amount of zero.
6. The system saves the order — Include Save Order.
7. The use case ends.

Alternative Paths

Postconditions

Subordinate Use Cases Diagram

Subordinate Use Cases

Activity Diagram

View of Participating Classes

Sequence Diagrams

User Interface

Order Catalog Screen

Name	
Address	
City, State, ZIP	

Order Catalog [Submit]

Business Rules

Special Requirements

Other Artifacts

REGISTER COMPLAINT

Brief Description

This use case describes how a customer can give feedback to the company.

Context Diagram

Register Complaint Context Diagram

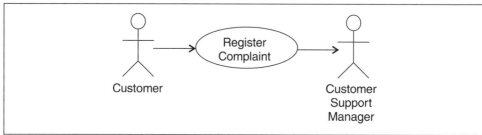

Preconditions

Flow of Events

Basic Path

1. The use case starts when the user selects Contact Customer Service.
2. The Message screen is displayed.
3. The user enters text.
4. The user selects Submit.
5. The system sends the text entered in an e-mail message to the customer support manager, and the use case ends.

Alternative Paths

Postconditions

Subordinate Use Cases Diagram

Subordinate Use Cases

Activity Diagram

View of Participating Classes

Sequence Diagrams

User Interface

Message Screen

Business Rules

Special Requirements

Other Artifacts

RUN SALES REPORT

Brief Description

This use case describes how a customer rep can get sales reports.

Context Diagram

Run Sales Report Context Diagram

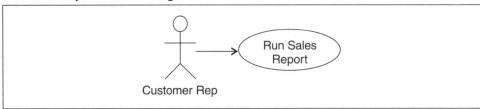

Preconditions

Flow of Events

Basic Path

1. The use case starts when the user selects Run Sales Report.
2. The Choose Report screen is displayed.
3. The user selects a report.
4. The user selects Submit.
5. The system gets sales data from the database (Subordinate use case: Get Sales Data).
6. The system formats the data into a report.
7. The system displays the report, and the use case ends.

Alternative Paths

Postconditions

Subordinate Use Cases Diagram

Subordinate Use Cases Diagram

Subordinate Use Cases

Get Sales Data

Basic Path

1. The use case begins when a request for sales data is received.
2. The system sends the month or quarter to the order database with a query for all the sales in that time period.
3. The database returns a list of all records found that match the dates submitted.
4. The use case ends.

Activity Diagram

View of Participating Classes

Sequence Diagrams

User Interface

Report Selection Screen

Business Rules

Special Requirements

Other Artifacts

FILL AND SHIP ORDER

Brief Description

This use case describes how a warehouse clerk gets information on orders to fill, their products, and the addresses for shipping.

Context Diagram

Fill and Ship Order Context Diagram

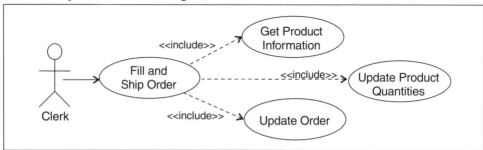

Preconditions

Flow of Events

Basic Path

1. The use case starts when the clerk starts the Fill and Ship Order Application.
2. The system displays the Fill Order screen with a list of all confirmed orders.
3. While the clerk selects an order
   a) The system displays the order.
   b) For all the items in the order loop
      1) The system gets information about the item — Include Get Product Information
      2) The system displays stock on hand information for the item
      3) If the item is not back-ordered and not shipped then
         a. The system updates inventory information — Include Update Product Quantities.
         b. The system prints the item name and quantity ordered on a packing slip.
         c. The system marks the item shipped — Include Update Order.
         end if
   end loop

  c) If all items are marked shipped

    1) The system marks the order complete — Include Update Order.

  end if

  d) The system calculates postage due.

  e) The system prints a mailing label with the shipping address and postage due.

  f) The system sends a notice to the shipping company that packages are ready to be picked up.

end loop

4. The use case ends.

Alternative Paths

- Inventory system not available
- Printer not available
- Shipping company not available

Alternative Path: Item out of Stock

1. The alternative begins in Basic Path step 3.b.2 if the item on the order is out of stock.
2. The system marks the item back-ordered.
3. The system sends a back-order request to the inventory system (subordinate use case: Back-Order Item).
4. The system marks the order "Back-Orders" — Include Update Order.
5. The basic path resumes at step 3.b.3.

Postconditions

Subordinate Use Cases Diagram

Subordinate Use Cases Diagram

Subordinate Use Cases

Back-Order Item

  Basic Path

  1. The use case begins when a request to back-order items is received.
  2. The system sends a request to the inventory system to place an order for out-of-stock items.

3. The inventory system sends an acknowledgment, and the use case ends.

Activity Diagram

View of Participating Classes

Sequence Diagrams

User Interface

Orders to Fill Screen

Order ID	Date of Order

Order with Stock on Hand Screen

Order ID

Product	Requested	Available

Business Rules

Special Requirements

Other Artifacts

RECEIVE BACK-ORDERED ITEMS

Brief Description

This use case describes what happens when a shipment of items is received for which the company has back orders. The basic process is to remove the back-order status from the order and the items in it. This will force the system to examine the order when Fill and Ship-Order use cases are executed.

Context Diagram

Receive Back-Ordered Items Context Diagram

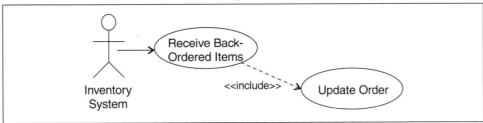

Preconditions

Flow of Events

Basic Path

1. The use case starts when the inventory system notifies the system that back-ordered items have been received.
2. The system finds all orders marked "Back-Orders."
3. For each such order loop
   a) For each back-ordered item in this order loop
      1) The system clears the state of the item.
   end loop
   b) The system changes the order status to confirmed.
   c) Include Update Order.
   end loop
4. The use case ends.

Alternative Paths

Postconditions

Subordinate Use Cases Diagram

Subordinate Use Cases

Activity Diagram

View of Participating Classes

Sequence Diagrams

User Interface

Business Rules

Special Requirements

Other Artifacts

SYSTEM ACCESS SUBSYSTEM

This subsystem handles login and logout, and checks for access permissions.

System Access Architecture

System Access Interface

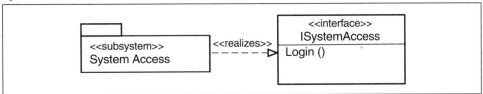

System Access Use Cases

System Access Use Cases

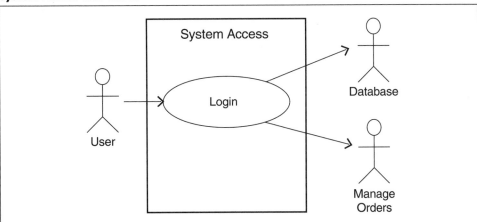

User is any human user of our system, which means at least Customer. We may also decide to have workers at National Widgets log in to the system, so that User also includes Customer Rep, Customer Support Manager, and Clerk.

PRODUCT INFORMATION SUBSYSTEM

This subsystem provides information about products. It interfaces with the inventory system.

Product Information Architecture

Product Information Interface

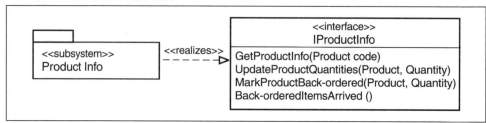

Product Information Use Cases

Product Information Use Cases

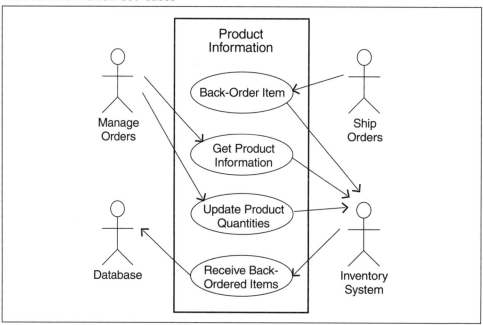

MANAGE ORDERS SUBSYSTEM

This subsystem handles order taking, product return, order status, and order cancellations.

Manage Orders Architecture

Manage Orders Interface

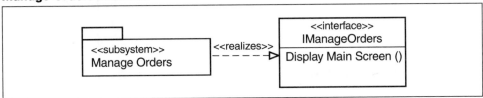

Manage Orders Use Cases

Manage Orders Use Cases

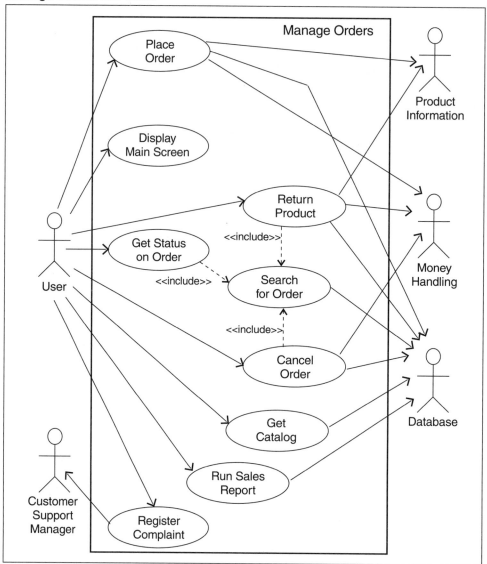

User is Customer or Customer Rep. The use cases the user is allowed to excute depend on their access permissions, which are set at login.

SHIP ORDERS SUBSYSTEM

This subsystem prints pick lists for orders, generates mailing labels, and calculates shipping and handling for orders.

Ship Orders Architecture

Ship Orders Interface

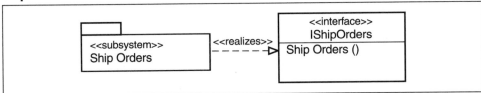

Ship Orders Use Cases

Ship Orders Use Cases

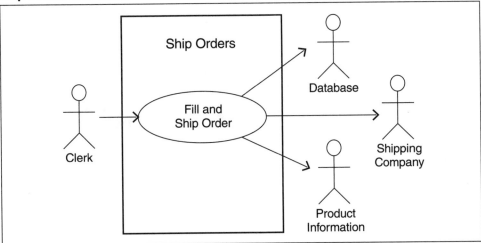

MONEY HANDLING SUBSYSTEM

This subsystem interfaces to the accounting system, updates accounts, charges and credits customers, and handles payment methods (checks, credit cards, and money orders).

Money Handling Architecture

Money Handling Interface

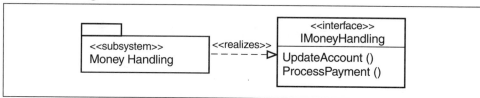

Money Handling Use Cases

Money Handling Use Cases

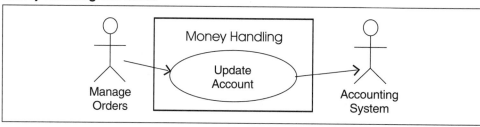

DATABASE SUBSYSTEM

This subsystem contains the data that we need to store for the application. It provides standard store, retrieve, update, and delete functions for the stored data.

Database Architecture

Database Interface

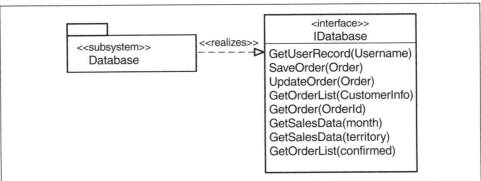

Database Use Cases

Database Use Cases

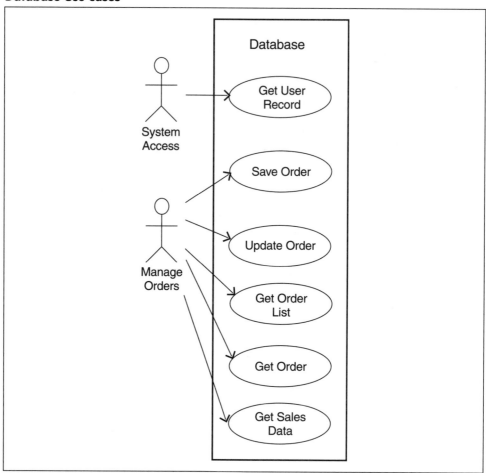

Index

A

Activity diagram(s), 67–73, 81, 91, 198
   template, 176, 177
   UML notation for, 181
   work flows in, 107–108
Actor(s)
   allocating to subsystems, 138
   alternative paths and, 59–63
   basic path and, 36
   in business processes, 85–86
   describing, 17–20
   documentation and, 90, 187
   identifying, 12–13
   interfaces and, 59–63, 61
   key abstractions and, 161
   sample, 13
   in sequence diagrams, 73–74, 133
   system boundaries and, 12–13, 18–22
   time as, 21
   weighting, 151–152
Ad campaigns, 167
Alternative flow of events technique, 29
Alternative paths. See also Scenario(s)
   as communication tools, 32
   completeness checks for, 31–32, 41
   correctness checks for, 31–32, 41
   detailing significant behavior for,
      40–41
   documenting, 42–47
   errors as, 37
   finding, 40–41
   in Place Order case, 39
   presentation styles for, 32–34
   project plans and, 148–149
   subordinate cases and includes vs., 141–142
   uses of, 37–38
   weighting use cases and, 152
Analysis class-based weighting factors,
      152–153
Application experience factor, 156, 186
Architecture
   basic description of, 123–124
   database, 237–238
   diagrams, 90, 175, 190–191
   dividing large systems and, 123–133
   example of, 126–129
   iteration schedules and, 167
   object-oriented, 126
   order-processing example of, 126–129
   pipe and filter, 125–126
   review process and, 101, 102–103, 106
   testing, with use cases, 129–133
   three-tier, 124–125
Architecture Diagram template, 175
ASCII (American Standard Code for Information
      Interchange), 151
Assumptions, listing, 8
Audience
   level of detail and, 81–84
   terminology and, 116–117

B

Back-ordered Items Received use case, 146, 153
Basic path
    basic description of, 35–37
    key abstractions and, 161–163
    potential readers for, 32, 34
    project plans and, 148
Behavior, significant, 40–41
Beta testing, 2
Black box testing, 164
Boundaries, system, 138
    examples of, 11–12
    identifying, 11–25
    potential problems with, 18–22
    scoping the project and, 23–24
Branching, 27, 29, 67
Bug tracking systems, 149
Build versus buy decisions, 149–150
Business processes, use cases for, 85–86, 107–108
Business process notation, 183
Business requirements, 120
Business rules, 91, 124–125
Business Rules tier, 124

C

Cancel Order Process, 73
Cancel Order use case, 33, 133, 146, 148, 153, 215–217, 234
    Includes in, 52
CASE (Computer-Aided Software Engineering) tools, 20
Class diagram notation, 182
Classes
    diagrams of, 163–164, 165–166
    key abstractions and, 163–164
COCOMO, 151
Code must be reusable factor, 154, 186
Cohesion, internal, 129
Communication
    across networks, 149
    interprocess, 149
    tools, basic path as, 32
Completeness checks, 31–32, 41, 101–103
Complex internal processing factor, 154, 186
Complexity, 152, 153
Concurrent factor, 154, 186
Conditions, 67, 69–71

Construction phase, 2
Context diagrams, 20, 176, 192
CORBA, 144, 184
Correctness, 31–32, 41
Coupling, loose, 129
Create Order use case, 162
CRUD documentation, 98–99
Customer(s), review process with, 103–104

D

Database(s)
    architectural patterns and, 124–125, 126–129
    architecture, 237–238
    dividing large systems and, 124–125, 126–129, 131–132
    documentation and, 94, 188–238
    interfacing with, 149
    key abstractions and, 161
    project plans and, 144, 149–150
Databases package, 180
Database subsystem, 133, 191, 237–238
    project plans and, 150
Database tier, 124
Database use cases, 231, 232, 235, 237–238
Data definition documents, 34, 92, 93
Debugging, extends and, 57
Decision points, 570
Delivery phase, 167–169
Demos, 167
Dependency relationships, 124–125
Deposit Sales Tax use case, 28–29
Design patterns, 133
Detail, level of, 79–88, 111, 117, 119, 120
Detailed Use Case Description Document Template, 90–91
Development teams, review process with, 104
Diagram(s), 91, 198–238
    basic description of, 67–78
    of the flow of events, 75–77
    interfaces in, 63
    sequence, 73–74, 91, 176, 182
    team collaboration, 86
    templates, 176–177
    UML notation for, 181
    of the user interface, 75–77
    work flow on, 107–108
Difficult programming language factor, 156, 186

Distributed system factor, 154, 186
Documentation, 27–49
  basic description of, 89–99
  completeness checks, 101–103
  of CRUD, 98–99
  Includes in, 51–53
  other documents in, 91–93
  of other requirements, 34
  of pre- and postconditions, 28–29
  review process and, 106
  subheads and, 27–49
  templates, 89–91, 175–177
  tool support for, 94
  traceability between versions of, 84–85
  Web for, 94

E

Easy to change factor, 154, 186
Easy to install factor, 154, 186
Easy to use factor, 154, 186
EF (environmental factor), 155–156, 157, 186
Elaboration phase, 2
  deliverables, 66
E-mail programs, 94
End user(s)
  efficiency factor, 154, 186
  review process and, 103–104
Enter Loan Application use case, 116–120
Entities, 160
Environmental factor, 155–156, 157, 186
Error(s)
  alternative paths and, 39–40
  basic path and, 27, 34
  handling, 148–149
Excel (Microsoft), 94
Exception handling, 40
Extends technique, 29, 51, 53–57, 85–86,
    113–115, 187–188
Extension points, 53–57, 97

F

Familiar with Rational Unified Process factor,
    156, 186
Fill and Ship Order use case, 146, 148, 153,
    226–228, 235
Filter architecture, 125–126
Find Order use case, 29, 30, 146, 148
Includes in, 52
Flexibility, 105–107, 126

Flow of events, 29–31, 35
  alternative paths and, 41
  diagramming, 75–77
  documenting, 90, 192, 196–197, 204,
    206–229
  template, 176, 180
Forks, 71–72, 181
For statements, 29, 30
FrameMaker, 94
Frequent Customer Discount use case, 55
Functionality, 27, 148–149
  basic path and, 36
  dividing large systems and, 129
  project plans and, 144, 148–149
Function points, 151

G

Generalization, 85–86
Get Catalog use case, 146, 148, 153, 220–221,
    234
Get Order List use case, 237
Get Order use case, 237
Get Product Description and Price
    Subordinate use case, 137
Get Product Information use case, 166, 188,
    204–205
Get Sales Data use case, 237
Get Status on Order use case, 146, 218–219,
    234
Get User Record use case, 237–238
Glossary of terms, 34, 92, 93
Guidelines
  for completeness, 34–35
  for correctness, 34–35
  documents, 93

H

Happy day scenario, 35
HTML (Hypertext Markup Language), 85, 94

I

If statements, 29, 30
Inception phase, 1–25
Includes special security features factor, 154,
    186
Includes technique, 51–53, 85–86, 113–115
  vs. subordinates and alternative paths,
    141–142
Industry standards, 150

Inheritance technique, 51, 58–59, 63–64
Interfaces, 59–64
    advantages of small, 62
    defining, between subsystems, 133–136
    dividing large systems and, 130–131,
        133–136
    expanding, 61
    key abstractions and, 160
    lollipop notation for, 133–136
    on use cases, 63
Interprocess communication, 149
Inventory System use case, 61–62, 232
Iteration(s), 143–151
    basic description of, 143
    length of, 143–144
    schedules, 166–167

J
Joins, 71–72, 181

K
Karner, Gustav, 151, 157
Key abstractions
    identifying, 159–166
    for order processing, 161–162
    in use cases, 160–161

L
Large systems, dividing, 123–142
Lead analyst capability factor, 156, 186
Login use case, 137, 141, 146, 148, 181,
        192–195, 231
    documenting, 95–98
Lollipop notation, 133–136
Lotus Notes, 94

M
Main Screen, 193, 194
Manage Orders architecture, 233–234
Manage Orders boundary, 233–234
Manage Orders package, 180
Manage Orders subsystem, 132, 134–135,
        164–165, 188, 190, 233–234
Manage Orders use case, 132–133, 137,
        140–141, 233–234, 236
Marketing, 32, 167, 168
Message screen, 223
Mistakes, common, 107–121
Modules, 124

Money Handling architecture, 236
Money Handling boundary, 236
Money Handling package, 180
Money Handling subsystem, 133, 191, 236
Motivation factor, 156, 186

N
Nested steps, 117, 119
Networks, 144
Non-functional Requirements Document
        template, 92

O
Object lifelines, 182
Object-oriented experience factor, 156, 186
Objectory AB, 151
Operation signatures, 61
Order IDs, 132
Order-processing use cases
    actor descriptions for, 17–20
    architecture example, 126–129
    basic path and, 35–37
    diagramming use cases and, 75–77
    dividing large systems and, 124–140
    documentation and, 187–238
    documenting CRUD in, 98–99
    identifying, 14–16, 22
    project plans and, 145–158
    system boundaries and, 14–20, 22
Order Products use case, 80–81
Organizational units, 86, 88
Other Artifacts template, 91, 177
Other requirements, documenting, 34
Outstanding issues, 91
Overstock Product Sale use case, 56

P
Packages, 180
Parsers, 149
Participating classes, 91
Part-time workers factor, 156, 186
Paths, 180
Pipe and filter architecture, 125–126
Place Order alternative paths, 39, 42–47
Place Order use case, 28–49, 59–63, 68–71,
        130–131, 136–140, 146, 162, 166,
        188–189, 196–199, 234
    inheritance in, 58–59
    interface in, 63–64

level of detail in, 81–83
sequence diagram for, 74
Place Telephone Order use case, 59–61
Place Web Order use case, 59–61, 179
    inheritance in, 63–64
Portable factor, 154, 186
Postconditions technique, 28–29, 90, 176
    diagramming, 192–193
    documenting, 28–29
Postconditions template, 176
Preconditions technique, 28–29, 90, 176
    diagramming, 192
    documenting, 28–29
Preconditions template, 176
Presentation styles, for basic path, 32–34
Priority, 90
    in risk analysis, 8
Problem descriptions, 5, 8
Product Information architecture, 232
Product Information boundary, 232
Product Information subsystem, 132, 188,
        190, 232
Product Information use cases, 232, 235
Project descriptions, 4–5
Project estimates, 157
Project plans
    basic description of, 143–158
    build versus buy decisions and, 149–150
    estimating work in, 151–157
    iteration schedules and, 166–167
    marketing and, 167
    prototyping and, 150–151
Prototyping, 150–151
Provides direct access for third parties factor,
        154, 186

R

Rational Software Corporation, 151
Rational Unified Process, 156
Real time systems, 34
Receive Back-Ordered Items use case,
        229–230
Redundancies, eliminating, 20
Register Complaint use case, 146, 148, 153,
        222–223, 234
Repetition technique, 29, 30, 67
Requirements analysis, 1
    level of detail in, 120
Requirements management tools, 85

Requisite Pro, 94
Response of throughput performance
        objectives factor, 154, 186
Results forms, 185–186
Return Policies screen, 216
Return Product use case, 146, 148, 153, 208,
        234
Reviewers, 104–105
Review process
    basic description of, 101–105
    for completeness, 101–103
    with customers, 104
    with the development team, 104
    with end users, 103–104
    for potential problems, 103
    risk analysis and, 102, 106
Risk analysis
    basic path and, 36, 37
    documentation and, 90, 188
    iteration schedules and, 166–167
    prioritization in, 8
    project plans and, 144, 149, 150–151,
        157
    review process and, 101, 106
    starting, 6–10
Risk Factors template, 175
Run Sales Report use case, 146, 153, 179–180,
        224–226, 234

S

Sales kits, 2, 167, 168
Save Order use case, 137, 200–201, 237
Scenario(s). See also Alternative paths
    definition of, 47
    documentation and, 91, 196–197
    document templates, 176–177
    project plans and, 144
Scope, 2, 23–24
Screen navigation, 114
Screens, as use cases, 112–115
Search engines, 149
Search for Orders use case, 210–212, 234
Seasonal Sale Price use case, 55, 56
Sequence diagrams, 73–74, 91, 133–135,
        176, 182
Sequence Diagrams template, 176
Ship Orders architecture, 235
Ship Orders boundary, 235
Ship Orders subsystem, 132, 191, 235

Ship Orders use case, 232, 235
Size requirements, 34
Special Requirements template, 177
Special user training facilities are required
    factor, 154, 186
Spreadsheets, 149
Stable requirements factor, 156, 186
Standards documents, 93
Storyboards, 75–76, 140
    reviewing, 103
Subordinate use cases, 136–139, 176, 193,
    196–197, 224–225, 227–228
    converting into included use cases, 142
    diagrams, 176
    for multiple case versions, 117, 120, 121
    vs. alternative flows or includes, 141–142
Subsystem Descriptions template, 175
Subsystem(s)
    allocating actors to, 138
    allocating use cases to, 136–139
    defining interfaces between, 133–136
    descriptions of, 124, 129
    dividing large systems and, 127–129, 132,
        133–136
    documentation, 90, 140–141
    in sequence diagrams, 133
Subsystem view, 164–166
System Access architecture, 231
    documenting, 95–98
System Access boundary, 231
System Access subsystem, 132, 190, 231
System Access use cases, 141, 231, 237
System architects, 32
System boundaries, 138
    examples of, 11–12
    identifying, 11–25
    potential problems with, 18–22
    scoping the project and, 23–24
System Description Document Template,
    89–91
System document templates, 89–91, 175
System engineers, 32
System-Level Use Case Diagram template,
    175
System-level use cases, 189
System Name template, 175

T

Table form, of use cases, 32–33

TCF (technical complexity factor), 154
TCP/IP (Transmission Control Protocol/
    Internet Protocol), 62, 151
Team collaboration diagrams, 86
Technical complexity factor (TCF), 154
Technical factors, weighting, 153–157,
    185–186
Technical requirements, 120
Templates, 89–91, 175–177
Terminology, vague, 115–120
Testing, 2, 34, 102–103
    architecture, 129–133
    black box, 164
Three-tier architecture, 124–125
Times, handling, 14, 21
Traceability, 84–85
Training materials, 2, 167, 168
Transaction-based weighting factors,
    152
Transaction processing, 149
Transition phase, 2

U

UCP (use case points), 157
UML (Unified Modeling Language), 3, 67,
    124, 163, 164, 170, 179–183
    packages, 19
    work flows in, 107–108
Update Account use case, 146, 206–207
Update Order Status Subordinate use case,
    148
Update Order use case, 202–203, 237
Update Product Quantities use case, 146, 148,
    213–214
Update User Account use case, 236
Use Case Name template, 176
Use case(s)
    after delivery, 168–169
    allocating to subsystems, 136–139
    basic description of, 1–2
    common mistakes in, 107–121
    complex, 34–35, 46
    definition of, 14
    document templates, 176–177
    estimator, sending results of, 185–186
    identifying, 14–16
    key abstractions and, 160–161
    level of detail in, 79–88
    one vs. many, 108–112

screens as, 112–115
too small, 108–112
traceability between versions of, 84–85
vague terminology in, 115–120
Use Case template, 176–177
User guides, 2, 167
User interfaces, 75–77, 91, 176, 193, 194, 199, 216, 219, 228
guidelines for, 34
screen shots in documentation, 91–93
User Interface template, 176
User Selection, 162
Uses technique, 188

UUCP (unadjusted use case points), 153

V
Validate Payment Subordinate use case, 137
View of Participating Classes template, 176
Visual Basic (Microsoft), 185

W
Web, documentation on, 94
Weighting factors, 151–157, 185–186
While statements, 29, 31
Word (Microsoft), 94
Work flows, 107–108, 165–166

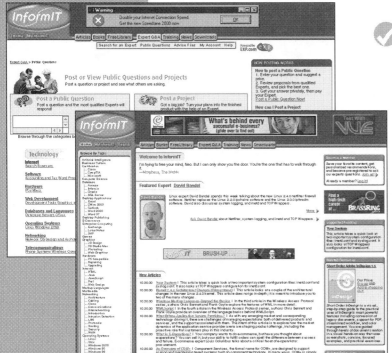